SCHAPELLE

The facts, the evidence, the truth

SCHAPELLE

The facts, the evidence, the truth

Tony Wilson

NH
NEW
HOLLAND

First published in Australia in 2008 by
New Holland Publishers (Australia) Pty Ltd
Sydney • Auckland • London • Cape Town

1/66 Gibbes Street Chatswood NSW 2067 Australia
218 Lake Road Northcote Auckland New Zealand
86 Edgware Road London W2 2EA United Kingdom
80 McKenzie Street Cape Town 8001 South Africa

A record of this book is held at the National Library of Australia

ISBN 9781741107111

Publisher: Fiona Schultz
Publishing Manager: Lliane Clarke
Designer: Tania Gomes
Production Manager: Olga Dementiev
Printer: McPherson's Printing Group, Maryborough, Victoria

10 9 8 7 6 5 4 3 2

I dedicate this book to my wife Elaine, who is my best mate, my soul mate and a truly top class editor. Without her help, patience, support, encouragement and professional assistance, this book would never have happened.

Acknowledgements

First, to Schapelle Corby herself, whose amazing courage and determination to still prove her innocence was an enormous and overwhelming incentive to write this book. I acknowledge her wonderful family—Ros, Merc, Wayan, Michael junior, James, Meleane, Wayan junior, Nyeleigh, Nyoman, Shun, Julianne, Sandra and Peter, and Melissa Younger, and I admire their strength and unity in this fight.

In memory of two great guys—Michael Corby and Greg Martin—you are sorely missed. And in memory of my dad, Arch Wilson and father-in-law Dr Ian McCready.

To my loved ones for their support of—my wife Elaine, my mum Shirley, and mum-in-law Muriel, whose advice in this case I have sought often.

Also thanks to family members Alison and Martin, Fiona and Jim, Debbie and Alastair, and John.

To my special friends—David and Karla and my goddaughters Stella and Grace, David, Nicky and Danielle; Feyne, Joan, Ellie, Kassie and Paul; Murray and Chellamah (Shelly); Mark and Cam; Cliff and Bob; 'Footy' Pete, Alan and Diane; Lino and Sue and the mighty Kay Danes.

Special thanks to former workmates Sarah Vogler for her amazing loyalty and backbone, both for this book and in the workplace, and Daniel Meers for his unwavering support over the past four years, plus all those brilliant young cadets that have graced the Bully's scanner 'den' in recent years.

To Fiona Schultz for believing in Schapelle and for giving this project life, plus a big thank you to all the highly professional team at New Holland Publishers, with a special thanks to Lliane Clarke, the marketing team and the creative design crew.

To all supporters of Schapelle Corby—keep up the good fight, we will prevail. Special mention to all official supporters, you are just great and the Corby family is most appreciative.

They can be contacted through www.freeschapelle.net which is the official support site or its Australian website—www.freeschapelle.com au.

There is also the Schapelle Support and Lobby Network—an International Network of Support for an Australian Wrongfully Detained in Bali, PO Box 1202, Waverley Gardens Vic 3170, Australia and its email address is: nwyndom@optusnet.com.au.

Finally there is the wonderful site of Kay Danes who helps the families of numerous prisoners in foreign jails, www.foreignprisoners.com

CONTENTS

Introduction

THIS is a truly disturbing story. One of the most frightening aspects is that it could happen to anyone. I am hoping that throughout this book, you will place yourself in Schapelle's shoes. Ask yourself: 'What would I do now?', 'how would I handle this situation?'.

Would you know who to contact if one of your loved ones suddenly landed in a foreign jail? How would you cope if your family was suddenly caught in the glare of a powerful media spotlight and they remained frozen in that revealing glare for years, with everything they did and said scrutinised and hung out in the public arena, often swathed in lies and half truths? How would you deal with the anger, the frustration and the complete lack of privacy?

Well, it happened to a person from my home city, the Gold Coast in Queensland and for Schapelle Leigh Corby, her family and close friends, the shock waves of her arrest in October 2004 are still being felt with the full force of a strong earthquake.

I began my journalistic career more than 30 years ago, with the majority of those years spent as a crime/police reporter in Victoria, England and Queensland. I have covered all manner of horror stories from grisly murders to tragic natural disasters with major loss of life. But never have I covered anything that has touched me so deeply and even changed the way I look at certain people and events.

I became involved in the story two days after Schapelle was arrested. At that time it was just another routine story, although I do remember thinking, after I had interviewed the late Michael Corby for the first time: What if his daughter is innocent and the drugs were not hers? What a truly horrible situation to be in.

Since then, I've written more than 150 newspaper stories on Schapelle and her family. I don't know exactly when I first believed in Schapelle's innocence but it was fairly quickly. Her verdict day on May 27, 2005, was one of the most difficult days of my life thus far. After I met Schapelle for the first time on May 30, 2005, I knew I had to do all in my limited power to help her and her family to tell as many people as possible the truth about her case.

That was my original motivation to write this book. As the lies and hype about Schapelle and her family mounted, and then seemed to gather momentum, that motivation became far stronger and it seemed more important than ever to tell the whole story as honestly and fairly as possible.

My involvement with the Corbys also gave me a rare (for a journalist) perspective that I had not experienced before and that was of a vicious and inaccurate media that has attacked Schapelle and her family, sometimes just because her name is a guaranteed newspaper seller or ratings gatherer, and even sometimes just for the sake of attacking an almost defenceless woman who cannot sue anyone.

Being close to the Corbys and being as involved as I have been, also meant that there were times when I was present at, or even part of, events that became news. This also gave me, as a journalist, the unusual perspective of not always having to rely on others to tell me what had occurred because I was privy to the events myself. I know the facts from first-hand experience.

This has made me a 'danger' to some people and there have been serious efforts to discredit me and make me seem less than the objective journalist I believe I am.

These efforts have only hardened my resolve for the truth to be told. And in this case there has been an incredible amount of untruths put into the public arena. I deeply wish that I could reveal who put the drugs in Schapelle's bag, but I can't and unfortunately I doubt that will ever be known, despite many people's claims. What I hope this book achieves is to tell of an average Aussie family being thrown into something more horrible than your worst nightmare, how everything has conspired against Schapelle and her family, with even their few victories coming at considerable personal cost to them.

There is a lesson in this story for everyone who ever sets foot on an international flight. But above all else this is about Schapelle and her fight to stay sane and healthy in an Asian prison, battling every waking minute to understand why she is serving 20 years—for having an unlocked boogie-board bag.

1.
March 2006

IT was raining as it only can in the tropics—with power, volume and relentlessness.

Everywhere you looked around Bali's notorious Kerobokan Prison, water was running or massing in pools. Some enterprising prisoners had buckets out to collect what is truly liquid gold in this place, where to take a shower is the stuff of dreams and running water is not to be taken for granted.

One prisoner had some of his clothes soaking in a bucket because this was pure water, while the stuff that came from the prison taps was certainly not fit for drinking, or much else.

The incessant downpour and leaden skies made Kerobokan more drab and depressing than usual. Visitors were thin on the ground as my wife Elaine and I waited in the visitors' area, with its dirty white walls sporting watermarks from previous wet seasons.

A large puddle grew beside us in the alcove where we stood looking out in the general direction of the women's section, home to Schapelle Corby who, like us, hails from the Gold Coast—Australia's premier tourist destination in southern Queensland.

Schapelle Corby had become a household name in Australia, after she was arrested at Bali's Ngurah Rai international airport on October 8, 2004 when Customs officers found 4.1kg (9lb) of high quality marijuana in her unlocked boogie-board bag after she arrived in Indonesia on a flight from Sydney.

Schapelle has steadfastly and vehemently maintained the drugs were not hers and had been planted in her bag by a person or persons unknown. She has never wavered from this.

Her trials made headlines across Australia; her verdict day on May 27, 2005 was broadcast live by two Australian commercial TV stations; news of her 20-year sentence also featured on TV, radio and newspaper reports in Indonesia, New Zealand, Europe, the United Kingdom, the United States, South Africa and other nations.

At the time of the verdict, polls showed as many as 91 per cent of Australians believed Schapelle Corby was innocent—an astonishing and unprecedented percentage.

As a journalist on the *Gold Coast Bulletin,* I followed her case from the beginning. Now, 10 months after her arrest, it was my fourth visit to Bali and Elaine's second in five months. We were keen to see her and to reassure her of our support and that of tens of thousands of people back home in Australia.

But things were not going according to plan.

We had arrived on this latest trip six days earlier on a Wednesday night and had made our way to Kerobokan prison on Thursday morning, only to be greeted with the news that Schapelle was too sick to leave her cell, or her 'cage' as she referred to it.

She was suffering her second bout of *mata merah*, or red eye, an Indonesian form of conjunctivitis that is 10 times more severe than the infection encountered in Western countries. It's also highly contagious, which is a real problem in a prison environment where if a prisoner sneezes, the whole jail catches a cold. Schapelle's sister Mercedes told me that when Schapelle had red eye in December 2005, she and her dad and her children all caught it as well.

'It's a terrible thing, very painful and I didn't leave the house for a week. It took dad and I two weeks to get rid of it, although the kids were okay in a few days,' Mercedes said.

'If Wayan had got it, no-one would have been able to take food to Schapelle,' she said. 'We were lucky.'

Mercedes had been living in Bali with her Balinese husband Wayan and their two children, Wayan Michael Junior and Nyeleigh, since the arrest. Their father Michael had also lived there for the past eight months.

The food for prisoners at Kerobokan is extremely basic and lacking in nutrients. Often it is only a wooden cart loaded with days-old rice stuck to the sides and filled with rocks and insects. All the prison inmates depend on their family and friends for food and clean water, which Mercedes would buy bottled and take to the prison. She is keeping her sister alive.

We had tried several times to visit Schapelle, unsuccessfully. At our previous attempt, Schapelle had sent out a note with a prisoner. 'Hey, Tony and Elaine, Yeah, sorry I've got conjunctivitis in both eyes. It's to (sic) sore, even to open them to write this. Maybe come back on Monday. Should be better.'

The inmates were not allowed visitors on weekends at that time.

So here we were again.

At a table outside the main entrance, we had filled in a book stating who we were, who we wanted to see and what type of offence the prisoner was jailed for. We then waited at the main wooden gate until the guards decided we could enter. They would often keep us waiting for at least an hour especially during afternoon visiting periods. We were never sure why they had made us wait—perhaps it was simply because they could.

Once inside the main gate we handed over our driver's licence or passport and a 5000 rupiah 'fee' (about 80 Australian cents) to the guard at the desk who entered our name in another book and handed over visitors' passes. We then squeezed through a large metal gate that can only partially open and had our bags checked by guards who usually asked if we were carrying any mobile phones or cameras.

We had some gifts from Australia plus antibiotic eye drops and face wipes we had picked up at a pharmacy in Kuta.

After our bags were checked, we crossed a big open space in the centre of a multi-sided building, then through another large metal gate.

Another guard at another desk checked our passes and we handed him another 5000 rupiah 'fee'. Then a trustee prisoner came to find out how many bottles of water we wanted to buy and whether we wanted to hire a woven grass mat and/or a milk crate to sit on for the visit.

Business concluded, the trustee prisoner then went to the cellblock to tell Schapelle we were there.

iI was the same trustee we had dealt with on the previous Thursday—Samsul—a rail-thin Indonesian wearing large baggy shorts and a baseball cap on backwards.

He had carried our message and food to Schapelle on the Thursday for a 5000 rupiah fee and indicated he was willing to do the same again for the same fee.

'Corby better today I think,' he told us and we brightened considerably, 'but she not come out in this rain.'

So we lent him our orange umbrella and watched as it and he disappeared in the driving rain down the pathway that leads to the women's section.

We watched intently for his return with Schapelle. It seemed to take ages, then suddenly I spotted the orange umbrella through the rain haze.

'Oh, no, he's coming back alone,' I said and Elaine looked crestfallen.

He had another note from Schapelle which said: 'Hi Tony and Elaine, I am sorry but it is impossible for me to come out of my bed today—the doctor or nurse is coming to see me soon. My eyes are to (sic) painful. I am sorry. Pelle.'

Elaine wrote a note to Schapelle explaining the usage of the eye drops and telling her we were flying back to Australia the next evening.

For more rupiah, Samsul agreed to return to Schapelle's cell with this note, the eye drops and the face wipes and we told him we wanted another note from Schapelle so we knew she had received the drops and that they hadn't suddenly gone on to the prison black market.

He returned with another scribbled note which read: 'Thanks Tony, Sorry can't see you today—thanks for the stuff + eye drops. Can't promise for tomorrow. Take care.'

We left the prison, unsure when we would be back to see Schapelle.

Waiting for a taxi to take us back to Kuta, my mind wandered… how had I reached this position where I had flown thousands of kilometres to see a woman I had never heard of 18 months ago.

A woman who had said to me a number of times: 'When will my innocence account for anything?' A question to which I still had no answer.

2:
The beginning

BUSHFIRE! The quintessential Australian disaster had been ravaging Queensland's southeast in October 2004, with five homes destroyed and three fire-fighters injured.

The Gold Coast had not been spared and blazes had ripped through the Hinterland suburbs of Mudgeeraba and Wongawallen.

The Gold Coast is a sub-tropical region and its bushfire season comes much earlier than in the southern states, often starting in August after the dry winters have created plenty of fuel. So October is smack in the middle of the season, which usually ends in late December when the summer rains begin.

As chief police reporter of the *Gold Coast Bulletin*, an award winning News Limited daily paper in one of the country's fastest growing regions, bushfires were a part of my job description, so as I sat on my back deck having breakfast on Sunday, October 10, 2004, I expected to be covering more fires on that Sunday shift as I had done the previous Friday.

As I munched my toast and scanned the Sunday papers, I suddenly stopped when a smallish article grabbed my attention.

Written by Cindy Wockner, the headline stated: 'Student faces death penalty.'

It said an Australian student—'Schapelle Leigh Corby, 27, from Tugun on the Gold Coast was arrested on Friday afternoon at Bali's airport in Denpasar after an X-ray scan by customs officers showed an unusual package in her body board bag'.

The story went on to report that customs officers found 4.2kg of marijuana in a large plastic bag inside her unlocked body board bag (called a boogie-board in Australia). There was some confusion later as to whether it was 4.2kg (9.259lbs) of marijuana or 4.1kg. It was in fact 4.1kg (9.038lbs).

It was mentioned prominently in the report, which was published in a handful of News Limited Sunday papers, that Schapelle could face the death penalty by firing squad.

I thought this story had loads of potential. It was a yarn tailor-made for 'The Bully', the *Gold Coast Bulletin*, so I decided to give it my full attention when I reached the office.

After a discussion with chief of staff Karl Condon, it was decided I would head to Tugun with senior photographer Glenn Hampson. It hadn't taken a great deal of detective work to find the family address.

Glenn and I arrived at the Corby duplex at around 11am and there we met an agitated Michael Corby, Schapelle's father, and two of her friends, Grant Ford and Troy Allard.

Michael's woolly hair and long beard made him look like a wannabe bikie and he and Schapelle's two mates were suspicious of Glenn and me. Schapelle's friends deferred to Michael on most of my questions. Michael complained that the media had been on his phone all morning, and he clearly had never dealt with media before. All three were quick to tell us that Schapelle would not touch drugs.

'It takes her a bloody week to smoke a packet of cigarettes,' growled Michael as he chain-smoked with shaky hands, the forefinger and middle finger that held his cigarettes stained dark yellow—the classic sign of a heavy smoker.

'No drugs. This is just a bloody set up somewhere.'

He explained how stunned he had been when told of his daughter's plight.

'I'm being treated for prostate cancer and I'm not supposed to have any stress—well, what about this for bloody stress. I can't even sleep and I know my daughter is not guilty of this.'

Michael Corby had been diagnosed with terminal cancer some months earlier and had been told that he had six months to live. The doctor had said it was too late for treatment like chemotherapy and he had been put on monthly hormone injections to keep his strength up.

On that Sunday when I first met him, he was upset, angry and confused. But he was quickly on the front foot. 'The first question I want answered is, with all this anti-terrorist checking at Australian airports, how is Schapelle supposed to have got more than four kilos past all those checks at Sydney airport,' he pondered. 'It just doesn't make sense. She's not dumb, she wouldn't try something so stupid and she doesn't have anything to do with drugs anyway.'

He explained that Schapelle and her brother James, then 17, together with two friends, had gone to see their sister Mercedes, who was visiting the family of her Balinese husband, Wayan.

'Mercedes is turning the big three-O and there was a crew going to celebrate. Now Schapelle is in the slammer,' he said with a bluntness that I was to learn was simply Michael's direct way of speaking.

I began asking him questions about what state Schapelle was in and how the boogie-board bag was involved.

'Mercedes is taking food to her in the jail and she told me the authorities are treating Schapelle all right but she shouldn't be in there. I watched Schapelle pack and she only had a few clothes, so I guess she was going to buy some there. I even helped mend her boogie-board bag. I even sat there while she put the boogie-board into the bag and I can tell you there was nothing else in there. She didn't lock it— she didn't own a lock.

Michael had repaired the arm rope connection to Schapelle's boogie-board himself and the bag handle had been repaired at a Mermaid Beach shop not long before the trip. 'That's why Schapelle was so annoyed when she saw it was broken when they arrived at Bali Airport, because she thought "Shit I've just paid to have that fixed",' Schapelle's mother Rosleigh Rose told me.

Michael explained to me that Schapelle had been really excited about her brief holiday to visit her sister before returning to Australia and her studies as a beauty therapy student. And looking after her father as he battled cancer.

'I had given her $500 spending money and she had saved $1000 herself. There is no way she would have been able to buy those drugs even if she had wanted to. The media is claiming the drugs would have cost tens of thousands of dollars —Schapelle didn't have enough money for anything like that! And she wouldn't be so stupid to carry it for anyone else. The whole thing is really suss.'

Schapelle's mate Grant Ford chimed in and said the case against her was 'complete crap'.

'She has been studying at TAFE to become a beautician and there is no way she'd be involved in anything like this, it's just not her,' he said emphatically. His words would be echoed by the many friends and relatives I would speak to or interview over the next few months.

As we talked, I asked Michael for a photo of Schapelle that we could publish with the story. He said there were photos in the house, but he didn't know where they were and he wasn't about to go poking about in Schapelle's room. Grant said he had one at his home and we agreed to meet that afternoon at a small shopping centre in Mermaid Beach.

Michael questioned me repeatedly about how I was going to write the story.

'What spin are you going to put on this, are you going to say my daughter is a drug carrier or what?' he demanded a number of times. I told him that was not my way, that I was just going to report the facts as I knew them, in a straightforward way. The next day when we spoke on the phone, Michael told me my story was OK. 'You did it like you said you would,' he said in a surprised tone.

Then Michael dropped a bombshell—something I still ponder about long and hard, among a plethora of facts about this complex case that just don't seem to add up.

'Do you think the cops will come to my house today?' Michael asked me.

'What, they haven't been there yet?' I said, quite stunned. 'I would have thought they would have been knocking on your door on Friday night.'

Schapelle had been at her father's place at Tugun packing her bags on Thursday before leaving to spend Thursday night with her mother Rosleigh at Loganlea. Loganlea is just south of Brisbane and not far from Brisbane Airport. The travellers had decided it would be easier to make the early international flight from there. Michael confirmed that the police had not been to either the Loganlea home or the Tugun home. They never went to either address in relation to Schapelle.

I found this strange. Ever since the first Bali bombing in 2002, Australian Federal Police (AFP) had formed a close relationship with their Balinese counterparts. They would have known of the arrest of an Australian on drug charges in Bali very quickly. The normal protocol would be for the AFP to contact Queensland police and then, armed with a search warrant, accompany the 'local boys' to both relevant addresses. As a police reporter, I have a number of Queensland police contacts, from beat coppers to the most senior ranks. Every officer that I have spoken to about this omission has expressed great surprise that the Tugun and Loganlea homes were never searched.

'I would have thought it would have been the first thing they would have done, it's the logical thing to do from a police perspective,' said one very senior Gold Coast officer, who did not want to be named.

'If she had packed the drugs at either address, with our modern forensics we would have found evidence of it and then the Indonesians would have been presented with an open and shut case. You really have to wonder why the AFP never contacted us to do a search.'

There are not too many explanations for it. Perhaps it was just an oversight, but that seems unlikely.

Maybe the AFP felt the case against Schapelle Corby was strong enough that they didn't need to get involved. Balinese lawyers explained to me in the first week after Schapelle's arrest that the drugs were found in her bag and under Indonesian law that was game, set and match. Conspiracy theorists have been all over the Corby case from the beginning and the role of the AFP in this matter has been questionable, to say the least, so it has to be asked: Could the AFP have not searched these two homes because they knew there was nothing to find, because they knew the marijuana had never been there?

It is a frightening proposition but it's one that won't go away, no matter how much time has elapsed.

I contacted the AFP media bureau in Canberra about this in October 2004 but they declined to comment, which in itself wasn't unusual. The lack of any search was raised during

Schapelle's trial, but like so many things, it was not taken into account.

Later on that Sunday, I met with Grant Ford in the Mermaid Beach shopping centre and he handed over a photo of Schapelle and repeated that she would not be involved in drugs in any way. I looked at the photo and rang my chief of staff on my mobile.

'Hey Karl, this Schapelle is really good looking, so that makes it a better yarn,' I said. 'I reckon this story has a few legs, it could run for a bit, and there is actually a chance this woman could be innocent.'

It was a typical response from a hard-bitten police reporter. That night, Schapelle's tear-streaked face was all over the TV news. I was happy. I had a good Gold Coast story that I knew would give me a few follow-ups.

Checks with Queensland police and the Balinese police the next day about the value of the marijuana were also most revealing. At that time, 4 kilograms of marijuana would have had a street value of $32,000 in Queensland and similar elsewhere in Australia. The same amount of marijuana in Bali was then worth about $A4400. Sure, we could be talking about a great deal of difference in quality but certainly not more than $25,000 worth.

The question this posed was obvious—why would anyone willingly take a product to a country where it wasn't even worth one-tenth of the value in that country? It was a question that would be asked frequently.

In my first story and many others over the next two months of reporting on the case, I included the possibility of a life sentence. I was then told by lawyers it was highly unlikely that Schapelle would face the death penalty, so I stopped including it in my reports. Most of the other Australian media outlets persisted with it until the verdict on May 27, 2005.

It was only after this date that I learnt no-one had received the death penalty for any drug offence involving marijuana in Indonesia to date. I can only guess that the misconception came from the Indonesian authorities.

3:
The flight to hell

THEY looked just like any other group of young tourists—wide eyed and alert despite the early hour, all excited to be going on an overseas holiday. Full of idle chatter and lots of smiles. It was just before 5.30am on Friday, October 8, 2004 and Brisbane's burgeoning domestic airport was already showing signs of another busy day. The quartet was heading via Sydney for Bali, a popular, cheap destination for young Aussies that had all the right ingredients—a full-on night life, good beaches, cheap drinks and accommodation and friendly locals, yet an air of mysticism that told you this was another country, another culture.

It was only a few days away from the second anniversary of the terrible Bali bombings in 2002 at Paddy's Bar and the Sari nightclub in Kuta which had claimed 202 lives, including 88 Australians. But that terrorist attack was the furthest thing from the minds of the young foursome as they moved through the front of the airport in the dawn of a cool spring morning.

There was Katrina Richards, 18, a trainee kindergarten teacher. She had worked part-time at the Rox, owned by Schapelle's mother, Rosleigh, to save for the trip. The Rox was a down-to-earth fish and chip shop in Scarborough Street, Southport, an older, working class section of the Gold Coast. With Katrina was Alyth McComb, then 25, a former flatmate of Schapelle's and her friend of four years. The only male in the group was Schapelle's half-brother James, aged 17 and a Year 11 student on his second trip to Bali. He had been there for the wedding of the eldest of the Corby clan, Mercedes, to her Balinese husband Wayan in March 1999.

The fourth member of the group was Schapelle Corby, then 27. She had not been to Bali for four years, when she had been on a special holiday with her mother, Rosleigh. They met there for two weeks after Schapelle's marriage to Kimi, a Japanese surfer, had ended in Japan.

Schapelle had also worked shifts at her mum's takeaway shop to help pay for this trip to coincide with Mercedes' 30th birthday. Not only that, Schapelle needed a break from her role as full-time carer for her dad, Michael, as he battled with terminal cancer. She knew the road ahead was going to be tense and demanding, and was looking forward to a holiday before she continued to help her father.

'We were all so excited,' Ally recalled. 'We'd worked hard and saved all year. I stopped going out to save. It was my first trip to Bali.'

For Katrina it was an even bigger first. 'I'd never flown before at all,' she said.

Rosleigh snapped a photo of the quartet near the Qantas check-in area. On the back of the photo scrawled in pencil are their Christian names and the words: '8th Oct. All happy go to Bali.'

At 5.33am at Brisbane Airport, Schapelle and the other two girls were seen by staff checking in their baggage for Qantas flight QF 503 to Sydney—three suitcases and an unlocked, two-tone blue, boogie-board bag. No suspicious bulge had been noticed in the boogie-board bag by anyone that morning and surely it would have been noticed and commented on by staff at the time if anything had looked unusual. The boogie-board bag belonged to Schapelle, who was a keen body boarder and looking forward to the surf at Kuta beach.

4:
Packing and tracking the baggage

THE quartet had stayed at Rosleigh's modest, high-set home in Loganlea, on the south side of Brisbane, the night before the trip. Just before leaving for the airport in the morning, Ally remembered she hadn't packed the flippers she had borrowed from Schapelle, so Schapelle had unzipped her unlocked boogie-board bag in the brightly lit garage and tucked the flippers inside, next to her yellow board.

Ally, Katrina and James would later testify in a Bali district court that they all saw the yellow boogie-board at that time and nothing else was in that bag.

In Brisbane, their bags would have been scanned for metal and explosive substances. But luggage was not checked for vegetable matter on domestic flights. Qantas Group General Manager Security Geoff Askew said domestic baggage is screened for explosives, but in 2008 was still not screened for vegetable matter.

'There have been numerous enhancements to global aviation security including here in Australia since 2000,' he said. 'However, none I would say were in direct response to the Schapelle Corby case. In addition to investigations by the Federal and Queensland police, Qantas undertook its own inquiry and found no evidence to support the allegations that Qantas baggage handlers may have been involved.'

In Sydney, the bags were transferred to the international section before being put aboard Australian Airlines flight AO7829 for Bali. Here they would have been checked with hand-held scanners, X-rayed, then put on a conveyor for loading on to the plane.

The boogie-board bag was too big for the conveyor, so it went into a canister with other similar items. The canister was covered with a canvas flap at the end, but not locked, and it would have stayed in this baggage area for more than 90 minutes until loaded for the flight at about 9.45am.

The area had no special security, just CCTV, and anyone with aviation security identification or an 'airside' pass could access this area at any time. Staff were not checked or searched as they entered or left Sydney Airport.

It has been well documented that there have been a number of drug-related arrests involving baggage handlers at Brisbane and Sydney airports.

In May 2005, as Schapelle and her bags were passing through Sydney Airport on October 8, 2004, it was reported in a national newspaper that Qantas baggage handlers were smuggling 9.9kg (22lbs) of cocaine, worth $15 million, off an international flight from South America. It was alleged in a Sydney court that the baggage handlers were paid $300,000 to see that the cocaine was removed before it reached Customs.

This so-called coincidence was described by Mercedes as 'spooky' but despite some major publicity in Australia, it was given no credence in the Denpasar District Court, and failed to be of any help to Schapelle in her trial and ensuing appeals.

An equally damning piece of evidence emerged in April 2006, when Sydney Federal Labor MP John Murphy revealed that two airport security cameras had been sabotaged on three occasions between early October 2004 and May 2005—again during the time when Schapelle and her bags were passing through Sydney Airport.

Mr Murphy said the cameras were located in the baggage area where Schapelle's boogie-board bag would have been. The cameras were the only security measure in that area at the time. He said he had asked the Australian Government as early as May 2005 if the cameras had been tampered with, and it took 10 months to get an answer, with the then Federal Justice Minister Chris Ellison finally admitting it was true in April 2006.

'If the Government had given me an answer when I first raised this matter and had then been prepared to send a representative and give evidence at Schapelle's trial, then I believe this poor woman could well have been freed because of the serious doubt this would have raised,' Murphy said.

Mr Murphy told me these details in a *Gold Coast Bulletin* interview on April 6, 2006. But by the time this revelation was made public, all major appeals for Schapelle in Bali had well and truly ended. Why had the Government kept this significant information quiet for so long when it was obvious it had a real bearing on Schapelle's case? Another unanswered question.

So in October 8, 2004, crucial security cameras were out of action and drugs were allegedly being moved around Sydney Airport, while Schapelle and the others waited quietly to board their international flight.

5.

Arriving in Bali

THE seven-hour flight from Sydney to Bali was uneventful. Schapelle sat with Ally and they enjoyed a couple of Victoria Bitter beers, read some magazines, played snap, listened to music and talked about 'girly things'. The flight landed almost on time, just after 2.30pm Bali time, at Ngurah Rai Airport and they were bussed to the terminal. At the terminal, Schapelle, James, Ally and Katrina joined long queues that quickly formed as the flights rolled in, to pay the $US25 arrival tax.

They moved on to another queue at the Immigration desk, where passports were stamped before the final baggage retrieval, and then into the Customs area. Gangs of nattily uniformed porters hovered and circled the carousels, trying to pick a tourist they could successfully approach with an engaging offer to carry their bags, for a fee.

In October 2004, an average of 5000 tourists arrived in Bali daily. The bags would have been on the carousel or stacked in rows on the floor by the time the passengers had cleared Immigration and the arrival tax area, which would have taken 45 minutes to one hour.

The four young Australians were tired, they had been up for around 12 hours and wanted to get to their hotel, freshen up and see Mercedes. They quickly rounded up their baggage and Ally noticed that Schapelle was struggling with her bag so she told James to grab the boogie-board bag, which was lying on the floor about six metres from the Customs area.

The strap on that bag was broken, which Schapelle and the others later insisted hadn't been when they last saw it at Brisbane Airport.

James dragged the bag the short distance to the Customs table. 'He was also struggling with his suitcase in one hand and his hand luggage in the other and he never even gave it (the boogie-board bag) another look,' Mercedes said.

Their bags ended up on the Customs counter of Igusti Ngurah Nyoman Winata. He asked James if the boogie-board bag was his and before he could reply, Schapelle chimed in and said: 'No, no it's mine.'

She said this in quite a breezy fashion, not knowing what was about to befall her. There are conflicting and ultimately critical views about what happened next. Winata claimed he asked Schapelle to open the bag and she opened a front pocket, saying: 'Nothing in there.'

Schapelle is adamant she opened the main part of the bag without being asked. 'I saw the plastic bag inside and then I reeled back because of the awful smell,' Schapelle told the court and also me later.

'I knew it was marijuana by the smell, but I had never seen it before. It was not my marijuana. Someone put it there.'

She has repeated that statement countless times since that day. Never once has she wavered. What is not in dispute is that Customs officers found a boogie-board, flippers and 4.1kg (9lbs) of marijuana inside her bag.

From the brief photos on the television it appears to be hydroponically-grown cannabis because of the enlarged size of the seed heads on the plant. However, the marijuana was never tested and has now been destroyed. The type and original source of the plant will never be known.

The marijuana bag had been shoved in near the top of the boogie-board bag and was inside two plastic bags. This was the only item of evidence in the entire case, yet it was handled by Balinese Customs and police officers at the airport. TV images clearly show them handling the outer bag without gloves on. More importantly, they also handled the inner plastic bag without gloves, which may have borne the fingerprints of whoever had packed and moved the stash.

Schapelle began pleading her case at the airport tearfully, with support from the others.

Meanwhile, Mercedes was concerned that she had not heard from them. Then she received the chilling call from Katrina that changed her life.

'I just kept thinking it had to be a mistake, Schapelle doesn't have anything to do with drugs,' Mercedes recalls. 'I was sure it was something we could fix and I didn't think it would be serious. Then when I got to the airport I nearly died when I saw how much drugs there were.'

Schapelle was crying and looked numb and shocked. But the girls felt it would be sorted out. Schapelle had to stay in the holding cell at the airport. So Mercedes left her alone and promised to come back as soon as she rang the Australian Consulate in Denpasar. She got through and asked what she should be doing to help her sister. It was now late Friday afternoon.

The Consulate read her a list of the names of lawyers who dealt with Westerners in criminal matters. 'I asked which one should I ring,' she says. 'I was told they could not recommend anyone, which left me completely in the dark.'

Naturally, Mercedes started to panic. She thought she had to find a lawyer that day, and fast, to try and get Schapelle released for the weekend. In fact, she could have waited until Monday, but she didn't know that then. When I asked her if she knew she didn't have to find a lawyer on that day, and would she have waited until Monday had she known, she said: 'Definitely.'

Mercedes started dialling. When she rang the first three or four numbers on that list, there was no answer because of the time of day on a Friday, so she kept working down the list until she got a response.

Finally she ended up hiring, sight unseen, a lawyer called Lily Sri Rahaya Lubis who, while inexperienced in cases of this nature, had a reasonable grasp of English. The involvement of her boss, Vasu Rasiah, ultimately proved to be a disappointment for Schapelle.

At the airport, Schapelle realised she was going to be locked up for the weekend. She was not only angry and nearly hysterical, she was frightened and in shock.

Later, both Ally and Mercedes demanded that the bags be checked for fingerprints.

'We got the same answer—too late, too many people have handled them,' said Mercedes. Despite repeated requests by Schapelle's legal team over the coming months and during the trial, neither bag was ever fingerprinted and they too have now been destroyed. If Schapelle's fingerprints had been on the bags, it would have been damning evidence against her—if not, it would clearly have been an extremely strong plank in the defence case, probably even a defining one.

James and Ally waited tensely while two more significant events occurred before everyone left the airport that evening.

First, Balinese Customs officers failed to check any of the other bags carried by the quartet, including Schapelle's suitcase and hand luggage, which Mercedes took with her when she finally left. Why?

The second significant event came as a dejected and distraught Mercedes was walking out of the airport. 'A customs officer and a police officer handed me pieces of paper with mobile phone numbers on them, which I gathered were their own numbers,' she said. She suspected they were looking for payment as a way out. 'I thought, no way! Schapelle is innocent! But I wasn't totally sure what to do, so I thought I have a Bali lawyer now, so I'll ask her,' she said.

Mercedes rang Ms Lubis on Saturday and asked what she should do with these phone numbers.

'She told me to throw them away, and although I kept them, I never rang the numbers,' she said.

6:

Schapelle
and the Corbys

SCHAPELLE'S has become a case that has involved her entire family as the media spotlight has focussed on them. This is not unusual in the cases of citizens arrested overseas—their families carry the entire jail sentence as well.

Schapelle was born on July 10, 1977 at the Royal Children's Hospital in Brisbane. Her mother Rosleigh is one of ten children and her early years were very tough. Rosleigh doesn't have a kind word to say about her own mother, and spent time in orphanages and years wearing hand-me-down clothes from her older sisters that were always ill-fitting. This led to many childish jokes at her expense. Through no fault of her own, she left school after Year 6. These days, she really only has time for her brother Shun (pronounced Shon) and sister Jennifer.

Pelle, as Schapelle became known, grew up like many young Aussie girls. She was enrolled in dancing classes as a child, travelled in her teens and 20s, loved a beer with her friends, and shared an affinity with the waves on Gold Coast beaches. Rosleigh said she was a perfect little babe, 'with a round face with beautiful eyes'.

'She was no problem, either, always a real good sleeper, sleeping right through,' she said. While Rosleigh was in hospital with her new baby, there was a woman in the next bed who 'spoke in a foreign language.'

'I don't know which country she was from but when she spoke to her family, the words sounded really nice. That's where the name of Schapelle came from, I wanted something no-one else had and it worked,' Rosleigh remembers.

Schapelle's aunt Julianne Corby remembers Schapelle as a 'beautiful, happy baby' who valued the strength and closeness of her family.

'She has always been much loved by her older sister, Mercedes and her older brother Michael and as they were all close in age, they grew up together the best of friends,' she said.

Schapelle grew up in a Housing Commission home in Ekibin, now Tarragindi in Brisbane's south. When she was a toddler, the family moved to another Housing Commission house in Christopher Street at Kingston, still on the south side of Brisbane.

Rosleigh and Michael split up when Schapelle was one and he travelled to north Queensland to work in the coal mines. The ex-Navy man turned auto-electrician spent 20 years at the mines.

Like most little girls Schapelle, together with Mercedes, dreamt of being a ballerina, donning a pink tutu and ballet slippers. From an early age, both were interested in ballet and other dance styles including jazz and tap, and they spent hours twirling in their bedrooms.

'Both she and Mercedes loved ballet and they loved to dance generally,' said Julianne. Their dancing teacher Michele Keane said Rosleigh took Schapelle and Mercedes to her dance school in Rochedale, south of Brisbane CBD, when they were both three year olds.

'They came to me for hourly lessons three times a week for

about five or six years, so we knew each other well,' said Michele. 'The girls learnt classical ballet, jazz and tap and they were both normal students who did exams and competed for medals. I can still picture Schapelle with that lovely smile going through her steps. She was strong-willed and determined. Rosleigh is a real battler, but the girls never wanted for anything.'

Julianne said that when the Corby kids were young, the two families were extremely close, thanks to the number of birthday parties and family gatherings. 'I have fond memories of kids' birthday parties at Charlie Cheeses, a pizza place at Carindale, south of Brisbane,' she said

Schapelle started school at Mabel Park Primary then shifted to Waterford West Primary—both on the south side of Brisbane. Her high school years were spent at Loganlea State High School with Mercedes and Michael Jr.

Michael Jr is a quiet guy and a keen surfer. He is referred to by the family as 'Splinter' or 'Splint'. Rosleigh explained this nickname came about because they often went camping near Tipplers Island Resort on South Stradbroke Island off the south-east Queensland coast. 'The only time we ever saw him during the day when we went to Tipplers was when he got a splinter from the wooden jetty there,' she said.

Schapelle also has two half brothers, Clinton (known to the family by the nickname 'Badger') and James, as well as a half-sister Meleane. Clinton's dad is also a Michael, and he and Rosleigh were together for about five years, as were she and James and Meleane's father, James senior, who is Tongan.

Rosleigh is very proud of how close her six children are. 'They are all good mates and they don't have many blues.'

Schapelle was a competitive runner and athlete at high school but the lure of the Gold Coast's surf was greater and she set her sights on the coast as a 16 year old, leaving school in 1993 and ceasing contact with her school friends. 'In primary school all the kids in the area would make cubby houses in the small bushland down the road from our home,' remembered Mercedes.

'We also used to love making up dances and Schapelle's favourite movie in her younger years was *Grease*. We used to make up dances to the music and call the adults to come and watch. Schapelle also used to make perfume from flowers and put it in small bottles.

'She would walk up and down the street collecting any flowers she could find and would spend hours a week making perfume. Schapelle also always wanted to do the food shopping with Mum. She loved food shopping and from a young age enjoyed cooking.'

Mercedes said the three Corbys learnt tae kwon do karate for many years at high school and were all members of the Bilinga Surf Lifesaving Club on the southern end of the Gold Coast, coming down from south Brisbane on weekends.

'All our life we went camping as a family at Christmas and Schapelle always loved Hastings Point on the northern New South Wales coast best,' said Mercedes. 'We also went to stay with dad up north on other school holidays.'

Schapelle's close bond with the Gold Coast and her years as a Bilinga nipper (junior member) and cadet (intermediate member) helped intensify her love of the surf.

Rob McCormack, a friend of 12 years, met Schapelle when she was a cadet at the Bilinga club. 'She was with a group of grommets (junior surfers) at the club, and she was, and is, a beaut chick,' he said. 'She's just a normal chick who loves the beach and the surf. Surfing is her thing.'

Many people I spoke to remembered Schapelle as organised and very neat.

'She has always been very neat and tidy, and was really fussy about cleanliness and having everything in its place, so we nicknamed her 'Grub', said her aunt Julianne with a wry smile of recollection.

'She always took ages getting ready to go out and she was really suited to the beauty therapy course she was doing,' said Julianne. 'It must have been really hard for her to share a cell with up to 12 other women and only one toilet for the first 18 months in Kerobokan, and even sharing with three or four others now, she would still hate that, as well as not having a shower. These may be little things but they would drive her crazy.'

'She was a serious child, but nearly always happy and quite particular about things. But she would do anything for you and she is very close to her family. She was really excited about that Bali trip because she hadn't been there for a while and they were also going to celebrate Mercedes' 30th birthday.'

She said when the children went to visit their dad Mick in Sarina in northern Queensland, their grandmother Pearl would sometimes go with them. 'They were very fond of Mum,' said Julianne. Pearl died in January 2005, aged 91, and Schapelle was very upset at missing the funeral. 'We didn't tell mum that Schapelle was in jail.'

Living on the Gold Coast for 10 years, Schapelle changed postcodes a few times, as is the wont of young people. She rented in Kirra, Surfers Paradise and then at Tugun.

In early 1998, Schapelle met Japanese-born Kimi Tanakam at a Coles supermarket, where she was working as a cashier. Splint said that during her teenage years Schapelle had spent some time working in Japan in a bar and she had surprised Kimi with some Japanese.

'They had fun together,' he said. 'Kimi was a character and very keen on surfing.' Three months after they met, Schapelle travelled to Japan with Kimi and they were married in a civil ceremony in the town hall of Omaezaki, a remote surfing town.

Schapelle found bar work at a traditional Japanese inn. Some Australian media reporters have tried to make more out of that but I have spoken to people who worked with her at the inn and it was bar work—pure and simple.

Kimi's parents were farmers and the newlyweds also did some work in their community on a tea plantation. But the marriage lasted only a few months—in the end there were too many cultural differences and Schapelle missed her family and her beloved Gold Coast.

'Schapelle wanted to come home, but Kimi didn't want to leave Japan,' said Julianne.

Money problems and jealousy contributed to the demise of their relationship. Splint said Kimi really wanted to work long hours and make some serious money and Schapelle grew lonely. 'Schapelle is a very social person,' he said. One Australian magazine tracked Kimi down in Japan in 2005, and he was surprised at her terrible predicament.

Schapelle finally left for Tokyo where she joined other Western women, working as hostesses in a bar, but homesickness kicked in and before long she was back home.

In 2000, Schapelle travelled to Bali with her mother Rosleigh to get over the end of that relationship. The marriage officially ended in 2003 and Schapelle, who was working two jobs—as a 'check-out chick' and in her Mum's takeaway shop, decided to enrol in a beauty therapy course at Ashmore TAFE, a northern Gold Coast education institution.

She was there for just a year and then, according to her uncle Shun, the family found that Mick had been diagnosed with terminal prostate cancer that had spread elsewhere in his body.

'She put her course on hold and became his full-time carer after he moved to Tugun,' he said. 'She still had one or two subjects to do and she used to study hard, but that was all put on hold, as well as most of her life after Schapelle, together with Mercedes, drove up north and brought Mick back to the coast. It's just a typical example of how this family will help one another no matter what. They may have some problems, but they are a very tight family,' he said.

Her marriage break-up and then her Dad's illness seem to have cooled Schapelle's own interest in being involved in a serious relationship. A social photographer at the *Gold Coast Bulletin* snapped some shots of Schapelle with her last boyfriend at a nightclub. Shannon 'Shagga' McClure, then a 27-year-old Gold Coast concreter, is also convinced of his ex's innocence.

'She is a very sensible girl and there is no way she is into drugs in any form,' said Shannon, who went out with Schapelle for two years. 'She is very outgoing and lots of fun and she had a great love of Bali, but I suppose that is finished now. She would be missing her life, family and friends.'

Shannon, who is also a mate of brother Splint, stayed friends with Schapelle after they split up and they mixed in the same circle. 'I wish I could talk to her as she probably thinks I don't care but I would not want to upset her or stir emotions. The modern Tugun pub was a favourite haunt of Schapelle's and another mate of Shannon's, Rob 'The Captain' Parks, who has known Schapelle for five years.

'She would come down to the pub with the boys and have a few beers, she preferred that to going to fancy nightclubs,' he said.

'We've all taken this pretty badly, we're dumbfounded. There is no way she would take drugs into that country or anywhere else for that matter.'

7:
Arrested

NOW under arrest and awaiting trial, Schapelle was taken from the airport to Polda police headquarters, about 4 kilometres (2.5 miles) west of Denpasar on Jalan Sangian.

The then Balinese drug squad boss Bambang Sugiarto said Schapelle was 'very stressed, crying and screaming' during her first recorded interview with police on Tuesday, October 12, 2004—four days after her arrest.

He said she became very upset as she answered questions through her lawyer Lily Lubis during a two-hour interview. Throughout those two hours she repeatedly denied she had smuggled the stash of marijuana into Bali, often sobbing as she did so. This was in complete contrast to early TV news reports and newspaper photos that showed her smiling, almost posing for the cameras.

Rosleigh and Mercedes said this was due to the shock and confusion that Schapelle was going through as she grappled with the terrifying situation she was facing and living. Her smiling to the cameras was as much nerves as anything else. Already, the media, especially the growing Australian contingent, was mentioning the possibility that Schapelle could face the death penalty and this continued to be widely broadcast until the May 27 verdict.

Schapelle was also not certain in her own mind in those first few weeks whether the matter could, or would, be resolved without trial. She and her family were confident her innocence would be realised and the whole nightmare would end with her freedom.

My early conversations with Mick, Rosleigh and Mercedes all led to the same conclusion—Schapelle was innocent and she would be home soon.

The cells at Polda are truly rank and the smell assaults your nose before you even reach the building—a heady, vile mixture of piss and shit.

There was no privacy and it was hard for Schapelle to find a spot in the cell to avoid the cameras that seemed to be her constant, unwanted companions. For almost the first four weeks, she was forced to sleep on the cell floor, because the police would not allow her any bedding. In her first TV interview with Channel Nine by phone on October 13, Schapelle said: 'I'm totally innocent, I'm totally innocent.'

'I put my suitcase and board cover on in Brisbane, you know, and I arrived in Denpasar and I had the shock of my life. I didn't know what was happening when I opened it. But I haven't seen that stuff before in my life.' The same day Schapelle, wearing a prison-issue blue shirt with the number 18 printed on the chest, was paraded in front of the media three times by police in what was believed to be a show of force in Bali's so-called fight against drugs.

At that stage she was reluctant to speak to the journalists gathered at the police station, but later, speaking through the bars of her cell, she said she had spoken to Rosleigh and Mick by phone.

'I spoke to them today and told them that I love them very much,' she said.

On November 1, Schapelle was again interviewed, this time

for a gruelling five hours. Afterwards she appeared wearing a prisoner's T-shirt with number 5 on it and her long, dark hair was pulled back, her face looking tired and strained. She again repeated that she was innocent. Through Ms Lubis, Schapelle appealed for the Qantas clerk who had checked her into the ill-fated flight to come forward.

'Schapelle's face was on TV and in the newspapers within 24 hours of her arrest and you would think he or she would remember her from that shift on October 8,' said Ms Lubis. 'And if the drugs were in her body board bag then, it's hard to imagine he or she wouldn't have noticed the bulge because the package of drugs was as big as her body board itself. It is ridiculous to imagine she would try to smuggle this amount of drugs through three airports in a transparent bag inside an unlocked bag. It just defies all logic. The check-in clerk from Brisbane could be very helpful for her defence and we are not asking that he or she comes to Bali. It would be sufficient if the person could make a signed statement.'

Rosleigh made her first visit to see Schapelle in November and told me when she returned to Queensland that she had fought hard with herself to remain strong.

'I couldn't cry 'cause that would make Schapelle cry and that was not what we wanted, so we didn't speak about what she was going through too much and sometimes we just sat there and said nothing,' she said. This was to become the norm between this very close mum and daughter over the ensuing months and sadly, years.

One day during her visit, Rosleigh shocked the police by storming into the cell area, armed with a toilet brush and toilet cleaner and gave the disgusting toilet a thorough clean. She was also photographed with Schapelle in her cell where Schapelle had drawn a smiley face on the wall—with the words 'Be positive' above it. This has almost become Schapelle's trademark and she often draws it on letters she writes to her supporters.

In those early conversations with Mercedes in late October and November 2004 she told me by phone that she had seen other tourists from various countries around the world, locked in the cells at Polda. 'They are there for a few days and then they're gone and we never see them again,' she said.

I suspect that what she was seeing was a shake-down or extortion racket involving Customs and police officers. I managed to speak to two other prisoners who had been through the gruelling ordeal and they agreed to speak to me anonymously.

They allege that Customs officers plant drugs on unsuspecting, predominantly young tourists coming through the airport, arrest them and take them to the filthy hole that is Polda where they 'soften' them up with interrogations and dire threats of lengthy jail sentences.

Meanwhile, they are cunningly asking questions to work out how much these tourists can pay. Then a deal is struck and the tourist victim is allowed to contact someone at home. Money is transferred to an 'agent' offshore (away from Bali, in Singapore or similar) and the tourist is then 'deported', told never to try to return and not to speak about it to anyone or they will be dealt with violently in their own countries.

None of this is officially sanctioned, but those involved are so traumatised, they will not query their 'deportation'.

I have no doubt this lucrative extortion is still operating and is an extremely good business for those involved, a sizeable group, with the average sting scoring the extortionists between US$10,000 and $US20,000.

During my investigation into this racket, I have spoken to a handful of Australian tourists to whom this has happened, an English tourist and a young male Scandinavian traveller.

Their stories are close to identical and all are too scared to be named publicly. One Australian tourist I spoke to went through this and spent three nights in Polda before paying $A15,000 and then being put on a plane home.

'It was before Schapelle Corby was arrested, and I still have nightmares about it,' the tourist said.

Others were so shaken by their ordeal that they didn't even want to be quoted anonymously.

From talks with these tourists, many of whom contacted me after Schapelle's case was effectively over, I found they also believed some Balinese lawyers were involved. I must stress there are many fine lawyers in Bali, but some I would never trust, and the ones involved in this extortion racket appear to have a dual role.

Firstly, they advise their clients that paying is the most sensible move, and in that they are undoubtedly correct. Their second role is to get to know about the tourist and their family, work out how much they can afford to pay quickly, then liaise with the police about the final figure.

Lily Lubis worked for Bali Law Chambers which is owned by the sturdy, Sri Lankan-born, Australian passport-carrying Vasu Rasiah. His business card claims he has a Bachelor of Science degree with honours as well as Engineering and English degrees from Australia.

When I first spoke to him he did not want be named. After that changed I and many others journalists assumed he was a lawyer and we all described him as a lawyer in the first few months after Schapelle's arrest. He did not correct any of us until early in 2005.

On their first visit to Australia in November 2004, Rasiah and Lubis came to the *Gold Coast Bulletin* offices to see me and they were photographed in the newspaper's boardroom.

During that visit, Rasiah said they were going on from the Molendinar office to see Michael Corby's duplex in Tugun. I thought that was a little strange at the time, but I was even more puzzled when they asked what I thought it was worth and I replied that I had no idea. They also asked Rosleigh similar questions about the value of the property.

During that first visit to the Gold Coast and Brisbane, Rasiah and Lubis also tried to get the CCTV tapes from Qantas of the morning Schapelle checked in at the airport. A Qantas spokesman told me that the tapes were erased on November 2, several days before her lawyers had asked for a copy, yet Rasiah told me they had made a request for them on October 14, six days after her arrest.

'We had a Qantas person in Bali who told me late in October the tape would be cleaned within seven days, so I quickly sent an urgent e-mail to Qantas asking that the tape be maintained,' Rasiah told me. At the time I believed him. I had no reason not to, but as time went on I learnt to take what everyone said cautiously.

During the early months of Schapelle's incarceration, Brisbane man Chris Currall was in Polda and then for a short time at Kerobokan prison with her. The then 37-year-old Bethania father of four spoke to me exclusively in April, 2005 after his release from Kerobokan prison.

He had been sentenced to six months jail after being found guilty of trying to smuggle more than $A1 million worth of pseudoephedrine tablets to Darwin in large flower pots. Pseudoephedrine is the key ingredient or pre-cursor in the manufacture of amphetamine, or speed, and it is becoming increasingly harder to source in Australia. Currall claimed he was innocent and had been set up by an Indonesian man.

'You could get almost anything as long as you could pay for it,' said Currall. He met Schapelle hours after her arrest on October 8, 2004. 'They brought her to the police cells at Polda and we were able to spend several minutes a day exercising in the small yard, but the cells were so close we could talk together all the time,' he said.

'She told me from the start she was innocent and that the drugs had been planted on her. And even at her low times she never changed her story and I know for sure she is innocent. That place was really terrible and I was in darkness for almost 24 hours a day with no light coming into my cell at all. Schapelle had a cell with a little light coming in but the conditions were still a shock. We used to talk about her case, then my case.'

While there are doubts about Polda police headquarters in Bali and corruption in Indonesia, there is no real proof that Schapelle was a victim of this racket. The biggest factor against this theory is the amount of drugs found in her boogie-board bag. If she was going to be extorted like countless others, there was no need to plant such a large amount of drugs, which lends considerable weight to the other theory that the drugs were put in her luggage by mistake and then missed when they should have been retrieved in Sydney.

There is one other theory which would explain the 4.1kg (9lbs) amount and still implicate corrupt Balinese and that is the decoy theory, told to me by three Balinese police officers during numerous visits. This is that Balinese Customs officers knew in advance that there would be a large quantity of drugs in a bag on Schapelle's flight—enough quantity to make a big commotion over—and that is exactly what happened when the boogie-board bag was opened.

While all this fuss was happening at the front and most public point of that busy airport, so this theory goes, a large quantity of hard drugs was passing through the airport bound for Australia and the Indy race carnival which attracted massive crowds on the Gold Coast later that month in 2004.

Following the Indy Carnival is the annual Schoolies Festival on the Gold Coast which attracts tens of thousands of school leavers from around the nation and this is also a drug dealers' magnet with large quantities of drugs being moved on to the coast every year for these two major events.

Through evidence in Australian and Balinese courts involving the Bali 9 and others arrested in Australia, it appears that Bali had become an Asian exit point for drugs destined for Australia at that time.

By early November 2004, Schapelle, her family and friends began to realise that she was going to face a trial early in 2005. Schapelle felt the judges would see she was innocent and send her home.

In mid November 2004, her situation improved when she was transferred to Kerobokan prison, Bali's maximum security prison. Australian Chris Currall was also transferred. 'I still saw Schapelle most days at Kerobokan,' he said. 'She was always so strong—much stronger than me—and I found her very straightforward and very polite to everyone. I offered her my Bible at Polda but she said she wasn't religious, but that changed at Kerobokan and we would meet each other three days a week for a church service.

'My cell was worse than a dog kennel. Schapelle's was worse then because she was sharing with so many people and the toilets were filthy. I'm not surprised she was often sick in those early days. I just want to see her home. She should not be in that hell hole.'

8:
The case is prepared from Kerobokan

IT'S about the size of a child's bedroom and at first it housed six to eight women.

This was Schapelle's new 'home'—one she still refers to as the 'cage'. It has a single drop toilet, known to Aussies in Europe as 'starting blocks' because you have to stand to defecate, which is no mean feat if you have diarrhoea. There are no showers, just a primitive bucket system. There is a basic light bulb, high on the ceiling, that is on 24/7 and it is out of reach to smash for those trying to sleep below its glow. For the first few months sleep came terribly hard for Schapelle and the family gave her a sleeping mask, but that lasted one night as it was too hot and the sweat rolled into her covered eyes and stung them.

The cell, naturally, had bars, but no glass in the windows which let in the weather and insects. Schapelle told me that some nights the crickets kept her awake, not just from their incessant noise but because they flew into the cell in their hordes and they would land in her mouth, eyes and hair. 'Some of the other girls in the cage would collect them, put them in a pot and cook them,' she told me on one early visit.

Schapelle was still in shock, but she tried to rise above the daily grimy existence she was being forced to live. Her illnesses ranged from chronic diarrhoea to skin conditions.

In the first few weeks after Schapelle's arrest, I mainly spoke with her dad, Michael, or Mick as he was commonly known, and then Mercedes by phone.

However, late in November 2004, a security guard at the *Gold Coast Bulletin's* office phoned me and said a Rosleigh was at the front counter and would like to see me. It was the first time I had met Rosleigh.

We sat at a bench in the gardens of the newspaper complex for quite a while and I began to get a more detailed picture of her family and my first glimpse of life in Kerobokan Prison. Rosleigh had just returned from her first visit and she showed me a number of photos taken inside the jail which were published in *The Gold Coast Bulletin* on November 29, 2004.

Rosleigh painted a grim picture of her daughter's surroundings and told me she was firmly convinced 'Schapelle would be home soon'. It wasn't until some time in 2007 that this mum stopped using that expression constantly. She is one of those people who loves to take pictures of her family at every possible occasion and her photos showed just how cramped was the tiny remand cell that Schapelle shared with five others at that time.

Later in 2005 the number in that same cell swelled to 12. The photos showed five or six thin mattresses side by side, so if you rolled over in the night, you would literally be touching cell mates on either side.

In one corner, the female inmates stored their personal belongings. There were regular searches and the guards would take personal items from the prisoners and sell them back to their owners the following day, if they could afford the price. There were no power points, no fans and minimal ventilation. With so many people in such a confined space at night, the atmosphere was suffocating.

Stealing among prisoners is a constant occurrence. In 2005 when her trial was in full swing, Schapelle was receiving a huge amount of gifts from Australia. The other inmates were jealous and even though Schapelle handed out a lot of items to the others, they still stole from her.

Attached to this cell were one filthy toilet and a wash area. Schapelle constantly tried to teach her various and changing cell mates about basic hygiene, of which most had no idea at all. She cleaned the toilet and wash area repeatedly, but few others bothered.

There are no showers in Kerobokan—just one bucket of water per prisoner per day. Most prisoners, including Schapelle, suffer skin problems because of the poor water quality. Outside the cell was a filthy green waterhole where the prisoners were supposed to wash their clothes.

The daytime offered some relief for Schapelle as she, like the other prisoners, was able to move around pretty much anywhere in the prison. But the nights were an entirely different story with the female prisoners locked in their cells at 4.30pm every afternoon.

During one visit, Schapelle told me she had suffered a bad night with little sleep because a baby in an adjacent cell block had cried incessantly all night. As soon as her cell was unlocked the next morning, she went around to this cell to see why the baby was crying non-stop. It turned out to be a cell that housed female drug addicts and she discovered that the prison authorities had allowed one of these junkies to have her baby with her for an overnight visit.

When Schapelle finally saw the baby, she was horrified to find the poor infant had been born without eyes and was also no doubt drug addicted like its mother, which probably accounted for the incessant crying. I could tell this had shaken Schapelle and it was just another experience of life in Kerobokan.

Another area of concern for Schapelle, who had never set foot in a prison before, was that she found herself sharing the prison with the notorious Bali bombers, Amrozi bin Nurhasyim, Muklas and Imam Samudra and 20 others. The main three were convicted and sentenced to death for their key roles in the 2002 bomb blast which killed 202 people, including 88 Australians. Just being in the same place as these fanatical killers frightened Schapelle, especially as they often heckled her whenever they saw her and shouted out her name.

Schapelle also spent as much time as she could with her lawyer Lubis and the chambers owner Rasiah, as they prepared her legal case. Early in December 2004, Lubis told me by phone that the police case must be finished by December 8, then the prosecution had 50 days before the case would go to trial, which would be late January 2005.

By far the most significant legal event during the pre-trial period related to attempts by Schapelle's legal team to have the cannabis tested. The origin of the cannabis needed to be discovered if they hoped to build an alternative theory as to how the drugs ended up in her bag. At 2pm, on December 3, 2004 The Australian Consul-General Brent Hall visited Schapelle in Kerobokan.

I have a copy of the file note for that date from Schapelle Corby's file at the then Australian Consulate General's office in Bali and it reads: 'The Consul-General Brent Hall visited Ms Corby at 1400hrs on 3 December and explained the AFP (Australian Federal Police) role, ie that the AFP have no jurisdiction in Indonesia, and could not be involved in testing (the marijuana) without a formal request from the Indonesian authorities, which Ms Corby said she now fully understood, but remained a little concerned that the Indonesian Police may not do the tests properly. Ms Corby then reiterated that she was innocent and therefore she had decided that it is in her interest that the tests be done. Ms Corby confirmed to the Consul General (Brent Hall) and Consular Assistant that she gives her consent for the tests requested by her lawyers (as attached).'

There has been a number of claims, even as recently as 2007, that Schapelle refused to consent to any tests on the cannabis which, it had been hoped, would prove where the drugs had come from, but those claims are completely false. The significance in her requesting such testing is obvious.

If the drugs had been tested and found to come from Aceh, for example, or some other part of Indonesia, or even elsewhere in Asia, then Schapelle would almost certainly have been found innocent and freed. If the drugs had been found to have been cultivated in Queensland, although not conclusive, it may have seen her serving a life sentence.

On that steamy December day at Kerobokan Prison, when Schapelle gave her consent for testing, she believed and hoped the cannabis would be tested. If she was guilty of taking the drugs into Bali, then giving her assent would have been a real gamble.

On December 16, 2004, in a story in the *Gold Coast Bulletin*, headlined 'Corby's life "a game"' I quoted Rasiah as saying the Australian authorities were playing games with Schapelle's life. He said they had hoped the drugs would have been tested the previous week.

'They are all playing games while this girl sits in jail not knowing what is happening about her future at all,' he said. At the time, I quoted an AFP spokesman as saying 'the AFP was still waiting for a formal request from the Indonesian police in the matter'. The then Australian Foreign Minister Alexander

Downer had asked the AFP to become involved for Australian security reasons to see whether the drugs had been smuggled through two Australian airports, which did seem a possibility. A spokesman for Mr Downer said 'the source of the cannabis is of interest to Australia'.

Federal police sources told me that the correct protocol was for the AFP to wait to be asked by the Balinese police to assist. 'We are a national police force, we do not appear for defence lawyers. Imagine if there was a drug bust in Queensland and the lawyers for the accused went to the Queensland police and asked them to carry out tests for the defence,' said a federal police source.

'And the other area of concern is that the Bali drug squad chief, Lieutenant-Colonel Bambang Sugiarto, has told us he keeps getting lots of calls from the AFP about the Packer case,' Rasiah said. There was a lot of AFP interest in the Perth millionaire Chris Packer, then 52, who was arrested in Bali on November 18 2004 for not declaring six guns and ammunition aboard his 55-metre converted Baltic grain freighter, *Lissa*. Mr Packer served three months jail for this offence.

Another file note from Schapelle's file at the Australian Consulate General office in Bali, dated January 7, 2005 stated simply: 'The AFP (Mike Phelan) then advised us that the head of the Bali Police had officially advised that the AFP will not be able to have the cannabis for testing.'

I spoke to a number of senior Balinese police, including Drug Squad officers, by phone at the time and then in person the following year. When I asked why they did not want an ID test on the cannabis, the general response was that the drugs had been found 'in Corby's bag', she admitted it was her bag and that was all the evidence they needed to gain a successful prosecution.

Many people may wonder why there was so much fuss about

testing the cannabis. There is actually a test that can determine where it has come from. In an ABC TV *New Dimensions* program in 2003, it was explained that in the mid-1990s, UK scientists developed a DNA test which could help detect cannabis on a person, even if it wasn't visible. Then it was explained that the then Canberra Institute of Technology forensic scientist Simon Gilmore had developed a procedure using DNA profiling of cannabis plants. Mr Gilmore, who had worked with the AFP, told the ABC program that his first DNA test for cannabis could tell you whether or not a plant was cannabis. 'But what we've been able to do now is to place cannabis samples within particular populations, say they might come from a particular state in Australia or from a country overseas and we're able to identify which country they come from,' he told the ABC program.

As there were no scans from the machines used to check through Schapelle's baggage in Brisbane or Sydney, plus no records available of the weight of her boogie-board bag, Vasu Rasiah and his team were placing a great deal of emphasis on the cannabis testing to give them a foundation on which to build a case. They also wanted the two plastic bags that the 4.1kg were stored in tested. In late December Lubis and Rasiah went to the office of Bambang Sugiarto to see about getting the inner bag fingerprinted because this would have been very telling evidence either way. If Schapelle's fingerprints had been on that inner bag, she would have been doomed. If they were not, it would have been a strong plank for the defence.

When Lubis and Rasiah confronted the drug squad director, he brought the bags into his office, said the inside bag had not been removed, then claimed he would have it fingerprinted. But this never happened and during Schapelle's second day in court the bag was removed and handled by the prosecutor Ida Bagus Wiswantanu and one of the judges, I Gusti Lanang Dauh. Even though the defence made repeated pleas for this inner bag to be fingerprinted, sadly it never happened. Now the drugs and bags have been destroyed, burnt in a public display after Schapelle's second appeal. It is one potentially critical area that can never be determined.

Photos and TV footage of the drugs showed that the cannabis had big heads, which is normally a sign the drugs have been hydroponically grown, but that has never been proven conclusively either.

By December 2004, and after two months inside, Schapelle's face was seen regularly on TV and gracing Australia and the world's newspapers. She was rapidly becoming a household name in Australia and Bali, with most people having an opinion on her guilt or otherwise.

Her first Xmas in Kerobokan was a low key affair, with Mercedes organising a private room at the jail for a family celebration. Joining Mercedes were her husband Wayan, their children Wayan junior and Nyleigh, her brother Michael and Merc's closest friend Jodie Power and her children. They were able to spend two-and-a-half hours with Schapelle and they gave her presents and ate special food. Mercedes told me by phone that in the weeks leading up to Christmas the visiting rights had been tightened severely after an escape by an American male prisoner who later was caught near the jail. After his capture, he was dragged back to the prison and severely beaten.

'We have only been allowed 15-minute visits with her through a metal grille which has not been good and Schapelle's spirits have been down a bit,' Mercedes told me on December 27, 2004.

'But she was good on Christmas Day and we spent a good time with her in a special room and we all sang and they respected her rights to celebrate Christmas. We were able to give small gifts like new thongs and underwear and I had cooked some curries and fish cakes and we also ate some seafood, so we were able to make the best of the circumstances.'

Little did they know that Jodie Power would publically challenge the family. Little did any of them realise on that Christmas Day that it would be the first of many that Schapelle would spend in that place. Schapelle and her family were all certain she would be freed at the trial early in 2005.

9.

A new charge is laid

IN early January 2005, Schapelle was again face to face with her boogie-board bag and the 4.1kg (9lbs) of marijuana. She was taken to the prosecutor's office in Denpasar where she showed the prosecutors how she had packed the board and a pair of fins. This was my first opportunity to speak to her.

When I rang Mercedes on her mobile on January 9, 2005, she was at the holding cell with her sister and she put Schapelle on the phone. I was taken by the somewhat girlish voice that I had heard on TV as she called me Mr Wilson, which I immediately corrected and told her to call me Tony. She thanked me for the support I had given to her parents and also said she wanted to thank the *Gold Coast Bulletin* for its 'fair reporting' of her case.

'Some media have already decided I'm guilty. Also thanks to everyone on the (Gold) Coast who is supporting me,' she said. She said she had been taken from her cell to a room at the prosecutors' office where her boogie-board, its bag, a pair of fins and the 4.1kg (9lbs) of cannabis were on display. 'They asked me how I had packed the bag and I showed them, without the marijuana, of course,' she said with a giggle. She giggled a few times, but I realised even by phone that it was a nervous reaction and that she was not being flippant. She told me how she met Perth millionaire Chris Packer in bizarre circumstances in a Bali cell that week. The pair had been put in the same holding cell on January 6, 2005 at the Denpasar prosecutors' office.

'We shook hands and introduced ourselves and the local media took our photographs—and I know who is the more photogenic,' she said with that nervous giggle again.

Schapelle and Chris Packer had been taken to the prosecutors' office for the formal handing over of their cases from the police to the courts—a move that signalled their trials were not far away. Mercedes then told me that it appeared that the court officials had been 'displaying' her sister. This was a common theme throughout the first year of Schapelle's arrest.

'They were walking around with her and the photographers and cameramen were following,' she said. 'What we thought was going to be an important meeting wasn't at all. They were asking her about her family and when Schapelle asked questions about the case, they told her to ask the judge. But it was great for Schapelle in a way, because it was something different to the way she now spends her days. It's amazing how the smallest change is something good for her. But she was nervous and a bit teary, so it's getting to her a bit now.'

Mercedes said the police officers in charge of both Schapelle's and Chris Packer's cases had shaken their hands and said goodbye at the prosecutors' office.

'It's certainly done differently here to at home in Australia,' she said. 'On the way to the office, Schapelle was taken in the front seat of a police car as though it was a taxi. But on the way back to Kerobokan, she and Chris and three other prisoners were all handcuffed to each other. It was the first time since her arrest the previous year that she was handcuffed.'

Assemblies of God Pastor Mal Feebrey told me he had decided to visit the jail on January 12 2005 'on the off chance that there were any Australians there'.

'Within minutes of arriving at Kerobokan, I met Chris Packer and he told me about the gun smuggling charges and how that was wrong,' he said. 'We had a good talk and then he told me there was an Australian woman there called Schapelle Corby and that name was somewhat familiar to me. When I met Schapelle she was sitting on the ground trying to read the Bible.'

'She was pretty distressed and we talked a bit and I calmed her down and told her to have hope and courage. Then she told me she was about to get baptised and asked me if I would like to do it and I agreed. It was a miracle but I got past about 10 guards and we went into an area behind the maximum security section and there were about five pastors there with 30 to 40 people from the prison. One of the pastors handed me a purple robe and then Schapelle got into the water and we did the baptismal ceremony and all the Muslim guys were hanging on the fence watching us, it was pretty incredible.'

Pastor Feebrey said he visited Schapelle on three consecutive days and her mood improved.

'She was pretty upset at first because she had been talking to some French prisoners and they were telling her it would cost her family $400,000 to get her out and one French prisoner told her how he had spent $65,000 to buy off his charge over one gram of coke (cocaine) and he was still there three years later. And that naturally upset her. I gave her bottles of water, a cap, some cigarettes and my wife's Bible and we talked about a lot of things and she had a lot of concerns about what will happen to her. I'm not thinking about whether she is guilty or not, only God and her know that. I just want to see her get a fair trial and I want to encourage Australians to take up collections for her family to pay her legal bills and, above all, I don't want Australians to forget her.'

The story I wrote about the baptism in the *Gold Coast Bulletin* was headlined 'Schapelle finds God in Bali jail' and it upset Michael Corby. 'What's all this religion rubbish,' he asked me the following day. None of the Corbys had ever embraced any form of religion and Michael said he didn't like the way it portrayed Schapelle.

Schapelle's first court appearance was due on January 27, 2005. The day before this, her legal team discovered that the prosecution had added trafficking to the possession and importing charges.

Prior to this bombshell, her lawyers believed that Schapelle would be charged under Section 78 of the law which only related to possession and importing, which carried a maximum penalty of 10 years jail and a 500 million rupiah fine (about Aus$75,000). The trafficking charge pushed the maximum penalty to life imprisonment or even death by firing squad, although that was unlikely as no-one has yet been executed in Indonesia over cannabis charges.

At no stage in the Balinese police investigation had they even looked at the possible destination for the cannabis. Police did not interview Wayan or his family, or anyone else in Bali, nor did they visit Wayan's family compound in Kuta. At the time, Vasu Rasiah said the prosecution was basing the trafficking charge on a statement by Customs officer Gusto Winata that Schapelle had admitted it was her marijuana. Schapelle has always maintained that she said that it was her bag, not her marijuana.

It is still very difficult to understand, even if Schapelle had made such a crazy admission, that possession somehow then could make a quantum leap to trafficking without evidence. During the entire case, no mention was ever made of anyone in Bali believed to have been involved in Schapelle's 'trafficking ring'.

The next day, Schapelle arrived at the tiny, stifling court house in Denpasar, handcuffed to an older woman. She looked apprehensive but determined. So began the lengthy court battle and media scrum that made her case into the number one Australian news story of 2005.

The pattern began on that first court day with Schapelle transported to the court in a caged police bus, with media following her every move. She was placed in a holding cell with about 20 other prisoners before being taken into court. She sat on a swivel chair, alone in the middle of the court room facing three, stern faced judges. Red-eyed and weeping, she said she was glad that she now had the chance to fight allegations of drug smuggling. 'I'm excited it's starting, I'm so relieved,' she said with a shaky voice. As she spoke, scuffles occurred outside the court as the Australian media fought to get in place for the best shots of her.

Prosecutor Wiswantanu made it clear to the packed court that he would only be convinced of Schapelle's innocence if there was actual evidence showing the boogie-board bag being checked in without the cannabis or footage or an admission from someone who put the drugs in her bag. But the defence did not have anything like that.

Wiswantanu read an indictment that claimed Schapelle had admitted owning the marijuana and had refused to open her bag when Customs officers located a suspicious package inside it. 'I understand it, but it's not true,' she said through a translator. 'I opened it myself. He didn't even ask me.' Wiping away tears with a handkerchief, she told the court that Balinese police had failed to test the plastic bags containing the marijuana for fingerprints and had refused a request for an ID test on the drugs.

'Because it's not mine and that's why they don't want to do it,' she said. One of her lawyers, Erwin Siregar, told the judges that there were errors in the prosecutors' four-page indictment, including listing 4.1g of marijuana instead of 4.1kg (9lbs). Rosleigh and Mercedes sat behind Schapelle and she turned and smiled at them a few times during the 30-minute hearing. The court was then adjourned to the following week and that became part of the pattern as well, with one sitting day each week until the end.

A few days after that first court appearance, I was contacted by a Scandinavian student who told me he believed he had drugs planted on him during a Balinese holiday in 2003.

He had remembered the scare when he heard of the Corby case. 'I had flown to Bali for a 10-week holiday and when I picked up my suitcase after the flight, I noticed someone had used chalk to put the letter X all over it,' he said. 'I don't know if it was this marking on the case, but I was stopped by a Customs officer and asked to open my bag.' The search was a cursory one and he was soon waved through Customs and he headed for his hotel. 'Because of the long stay, I took everything out of my bag and put it in drawers. Then I put what I thought was an empty suitcase in a cupboard and forgot about it. I didn't touch it again until I was ready to pack up for the trip home and as I was repacking my case, I spotted a plastic bag hidden in it. 'The bag was full of white powder. I'd never seen it before and had no idea how it came to be in my case.'

He said he threw the plastic bag and contents in a rubbish bin before he headed to Bali Airport.

'It was only on the flight home that I began thinking about it seriously and I remembered that Indonesia has capital punishment for drug smuggling,' he said. 'When I realised how I could have been in serious trouble, I began shaking. Now I wonder if the X on my bag had been put there as a signal for someone who could plant this bag of white powder that was almost certainly drugs.' He contacted Schapelle's lawyers and they asked him to supply a statutory declaration which he sent to Bali and it was used in her case.

Day two of Schapelle's trial on February 3, 2005 saw Customs officer Gusti Ngurah Nyoman Winata give his evidence. He told the court he was operating an X-ray machine when he saw a suspicious looking package in the body board bag. When Schapelle's brother James dragged the body board bag to his counter, Winata said he asked Schapelle to open it, but she only unzipped the front pocket. He claimed he opened the main zip himself. 'When I opened it a bit, she yelled "No",' he said.

'I asked "Why" and she said "I have some" and looked confused,' he said.

He then said that he took Schapelle to a room where he opened the bag fully to reveal the body board, a pair of fins and the plastic bag with the large cache of marijuana inside. Winata said Schapelle had identified the drugs, allegedly saying: 'I knew that was marijuana when you opened that at the inspection counter.'

Schapelle shook her head constantly throughout Winata's testimony. A second Customs officer, Komang Gelgel, backed up Winata's version of the events on October 8, 2004 despite not being present for the alleged initial exchange. Chief Judge Linton Sirait asked Schapelle whether she had tried to prevent Winata opening her bag and Schapelle jumped to her feet and angrily replied: 'Absolutely not. He's lying.'

She said she had opened the bag without any prompting by Winata because she saw other passengers doing that as well. 'I was not suspicious-looking or acting restless,' she said in a trembling voice. 'I was happy because I was on holiday and I love Bali. I open it, I lift it up and I'm surprised, there's a plastic bag and half open and I'm like "Ohhhh". And I close it up. I can smell it. I never at any stage, stated that the marijuana belongs to me... never, ever, have I stated that.'

Schapelle said she had asked Winata to fingerprint the bag containing the marijuana before he handled it, but he refused and then he and other officials handled the bag and its contents. The first TV footage of Schapelle's arrest supported her words as both Customs officers and police office officers swarmed around the table where the drugs and bag were sitting, repeatedly handling it and showing it to the cameras.

When the court asked Winata to show how the drugs were placed in the boogie-board bag, he put them in the opposite way to the photos that were taken on the day, but denied he had made a mistake. The cannabis stash was in a bag with a nozzle so that the air could be forced out and the package constricted. The Customs photos showed the bag placed upside down inside a second identical bag. Schapelle told the court that someone else had opened and closed her bag since she had last done it as the two zips were meeting in the middle whereas she always zipped it shut with one zip from left to right.

Winata's testimony was extremely damaging to Schapelle's case. I tried to have a conversation with Winata at his workstation at Bali Airport. It was virtually impossible as his English was basic at best, not even to the standard of speaking in properly constructed sentences. It would have been impossible for him to have fully understood what Schapelle or any other English-speaking person was saying to him in any given situation.

I felt it was a major mistake by Schapelle's original legal team that they did not make more of Winata's deficiency in English. Having said that, the judges were not generally proficient in English either, so whether showing Winata's poor grasp of the language would have meant much to those judges is questionable, but the public mileage could have been significant.

On her third appearance on February 11, 2005, Schapelle broke down and pleaded with the judges to help her escape the death penalty. Schapelle said there must be evidence available somewhere that proves her innocence to authorities. 'Isn't there a camera to say that... to help me prove my life,' she pleaded tearfully. 'If it's the death sentence, don't they have something to help me here.'

Two police officers who were the first on the scene then supported the evidence of the Customs officers. The court heard from senior Customs officer Bernandus Sutjipto who defended the investigation of his officers, although he admitted the drugs could have come from anywhere, including Australia, Pakistan or Peru.

Defence lawyer Erwin Siregar, who seemed to be doing more of the court work than the less experienced Lily Lubis, asked the court to check Bali Airport security cameras from that day to prove the officers were lying and the judges promised to take up the issue at the next hearing on February 17.

There was no talk of security cameras at this hearing, however, and the day will be remembered for the clash between Schapelle's mum Rosleigh and a group of anti-drug demonstrators demanding the death penalty. The dozen or so demonstrators from GRANAT, an Indonesian anti-narcotics group, invaded the courtroom shouting for Schapelle to be executed. They had placards including one showing an axe dripping blood and saying: 'The Death Penalty For Those Who Bring Drugs To Bali'. It was put in a window behind Schapelle's head and remained there for most of the hearing. Another placard said 'Quickly Execute Corby.'

This prompted an angry Rosleigh to shout at the protestors: 'How much did you get paid to write those terrible signs. You must be a bad person.' She then sprayed the demonstrators with a water bottle. 'You have found my daughter guilty and she is innocent,' yelled Rosleigh. 'Why can't you be saying try and find evidence. No-one seems to be trying to find who put the bloody stuff in the bag. They don't care.'

The Indonesian media who were covering this case heavily, made a big splash with this incident. Both in Bali and Jakarta, Schapelle was headline news, often being referred to as 'Ratu Marijuana' or Marijuana Queen. Court registrar Made Sukarta said the judges made no request for increased security at the next hearing on March 3 because 'they walked out in safety' after the water bottle throwing incident. This was despite the media scrum that hampered Schapelle from communicating with her family in any privacy at all.

The defence began its case on March 3, 2005, with Schapelle's travelling partners called to give evidence. Alyth McComb, the Gold Coast bartender and friend of Schapelle's for four years, told the court that there was no marijuana in Schapelle's boogie-board bag when she left Australia for Bali in October 2004. She said Schapelle had packed her board bag in front of her three fellow travellers and Rosleigh on the morning of the flight.

She said she handed a pair of flippers to Schapelle as she packed in a downstairs room/garage with another friend, Katrina Richards, and Schapelle's then 17-year-old brother James.

Alyth told the Denpasar court that Schapelle had opened the boogie-board bag right up and it was obvious to all those present that there was nothing else in the bag. Becoming tearful, Alyth said that Schapelle had never dealt in or used drugs. She said it would have been impossible for anyone to slip anything into the boogie-board bag before it was checked in at Brisbane Airport, which was the last time they saw their luggage until they reached Bali.

Katrina and James then gave evidence, supporting Alyth's version of events. James who, along with Schapelle, had been taken into a small room at the airport for questioning on October 8, 2004, said Schapelle never at any stage claimed ownership of the marijuana to Customs officers or airport police. He said his sister opened her bag voluntarily and never tried to stop Customs officers from doing it.

University of Indonesia lawyer and Professor Loebby Lukman also took the stand that day. Professor Lukman had helped draft Indonesia's tough drug laws and he was asked if a person could be convicted of drug smuggling if they did not know the drugs were in their bag.

'If there was no intention to import, and if she was used by others, then she should be freed,' he replied.

10:
Enter the
'white knights'

AT the back of the prosecutor's court in early March two men, keenly watched the proceedings. Gold Coast mobile phone businessman Ron Bakir and Gold Coast lawyer Robin Tampoe appeared from nowhere into the case. Rosleigh and Michael Corby senior are vague about when and how the pair emerged, because they had very little to do with them, then or at any stage. But they have always both been adamant that Bakir and Tampoe were not invited to become involved—they just appeared after getting in touch with Mercedes in Bali.

In Bali, the media exposure of the case meant that Mercedes was swamped by people with offers of help. She said at the time that their offer of help seemed genuine and was appreciated.

Both she and Schapelle knew of Bakir because of the plethora of 'Mad Ron' TV ads on Gold Coast TV, flogging his mobile phone business. Bakir was also a well-known figure on the Gold Coast nightclub scene, but both sisters are certain they had never met either him or Tampoe before late February 2005 in Bali.

Robin Tampoe was a lawyer of Irish and Sri Lankan heritage. He is currently not practising law in Queensland, but he used to mainly deal with cases at magistrates' court level. Lawyers I have spoken to with experience in foreign courts said he could have been a 'fish out of water' in Bali. At the time he became involved with Schapelle's case, he was a founding partner of Hoolihans, a Gold Coast law firm, which no longer exists. He had a far smaller public profile than Bakir, but he was also a businessman with varied interests offshore including in Indonesia, Pakistan, Afghanistan, Japan and South Korea.

Bakir's life, prior to his involvement with this case, has been far more public and documented. He was born Rani Muhuddine Hassan in Lebanon on April 21, 1977. Together with his parents, three brothers and two sisters, he moved to Australia in 1982, settling in Sydney, where they took over the running of a takeaway shop. His parents later divorced and as a teenager, Ron used his mother's maiden surname of Bakir.

When he moved to the Gold Coast he was using the name of Ronny Hassan and was renting an apartment in the suburb of Paradise Waters. He went into the mobile phone business, setting up a company called Ronicom International. The business made millions and he owned a number of Gold Coast properties he was operating with his partner and fiancé, Joenny Doueihi. They had a bitter separation in 2000 that ended up in a civil court.

Despite the pair's high profile involvement in the case, Tampoe and Bakir were of questionable value to Schapelle's case. I reported on Bakir and Tampoe and I, like other media, originally referred to Bakir as the 'white knight' and the person who (he claimed) was 'funding her defence case'—a claim which has never been proven.

I remember Rosleigh telling me that the family had not invited Bakir or Tampoe to help in the first place, and they hadn't really wanted them involved, but if they helped Mercedes at all, and took some of the immense pressure off her at the time, then that was okay.

I could tell that Rosleigh, with years of street smarts behind her, was suspicious of their motives. They pretty much gave her a wide berth. Ron is a salesman, who nearly always speaks as though he's on fast forward and there is something important happening or about to happen.

I remember driving to Brisbane with him and Vasu Rasiah, with Ron behind the wheel of a black BMW. We were going to meet with the Queensland Opposition Leader Lawrence Springborg, who was one of the few politicians to ever publicly support Schapelle (which he did that day). Bakir was talking alot about the case and what he was going to do to fix it.

Bakir and Tampoe denied knowing Rasiah before Schapelle's arrest, as does Rasiah of them, but Tampoe and Rasiah's families were from the same Sri Lankan area.

I can imagine Schapelle initially being impressed by Bakir and Tampoe. The case was not looking good even in those early days and Schapelle had been in jail for almost five months.

They arrived in Bali during the last week of February and had been meeting Schapelle and her Balinese legal team daily. In a media report on March 3, 2005, Bakir described Schapelle as 'one tough girl' who was enduring atrocious conditions. Tampoe said the Australian Foreign Affairs Department was now co-operating as they tried to track her movements through two Australian airports. He said there were a number of 'serious questions' that needed to be established before her trial continued. 'This is where we can really help and we are starting to make some inroads so we can provide the best defence we possibly can,' he said.

Early March 2005 also saw the Australian Government become more involved after repeated claims by Schapelle's defence team that they were not doing enough to help her. The then Prime Minister John Howard said he was taking a personal interest in her case and the Foreign Minister of the day, Alexander Downer said on ABC radio: 'We are concerned about this case and we are following it very closely.'

Foreign Minister Downer said he would meet with Schapelle's lawyers. Prime Minister Howard, speaking on Sydney Radio 2GB, emphasised that the Australian Government could not interfere with the process in Indonesia.

'I choose my words carefully because I have to respect the legal system of another country,' he said. The then Federal Opposition leader Kim Beazley also had concerns about the case, but placed his faith in Indonesian justice. Tampoe and Bakir met with Downer on March 5, 2005 with Bakir saying Mr Downer had given '100 per cent support' in their attempts to secure vital information from Australian Customs and Qantas. 'I think the meeting was very productive,' said Bakir. 'Mr Downer made it clear he will do everything in his power to provide the information we have requested. It is crucial we get this type of evidence. We are not talking about a great deal of time. If Mr Downer is a man of his word, and I think he is, we can really make some inroads with our defence case.'

Mr Downer warned them that they needed to be realistic about what was possible. 'It's very important to have a sense of realistic expectations of what the government can do,' he said. 'They want information from airlines, they want information from the airport and so on and where that information is not available there is nothing we can do about it.' He also told the men there was no point in lashing out at the Indonesian or Australian governments or authorities.

'The important thing is to concentrate on the case itself and to ensure that the defence argues its case as best it possibly can, not to attack the people who, in the end, are likely to be helpful,' he said.

Mr Downer said the men had wanted to find out the weight of the boogie-board when it was checked in. 'Well, that information isn't available because the boogie-board was checked in with other luggage, so there is only an aggregate weight,' he said. That information had already come to light before Bakir and Tampoe arrived on the scene. Mr Downer also said Bakir and Tampoe wanted information from the airport's CCTV, but he explained that the closed circuit system is wiped after a certain period.

About the same time, Mick Corby senior told me that Rosleigh had returned to Australia and had spoken about being approached at the March 3 hearing by the same Balinese anti-drug crusaders that had invaded the court the previous month with placards and shouting slogans, wanting the death penalty for Schapelle. 'They came up to Rosleigh and apologised to her,' he said. 'They said they felt bad and that they hadn't been able to sleep because of what they had done. They said they were now praying for Schapelle and Rosleigh.'

Schapelle's family was concerned about the appalling living conditions in Kerobokan prison. 'If she gets sick in there, she won't get better in there,' her father said. 'It's a slow process, but she'll be coming home soon. We don't talk about the worst possible scenario.'

The five court appearances had generated enormous media coverage in Australia by March 2005 and Schapelle had gained celebrity status, while her family struggled to cope with the exposure.

By early March, more than 3000 people, including high-profile professional surfers Sunny Garcia and Tom Carroll, had signed a Gold Coast-originated and based petition to free Schapelle.

A strong Schapelle supporter, Gold Coaster Guy Pilgrim had gathered the signatures and sent copies of the petition to both the Australian and Indonesian governments. The *Gold Coast Bulletin* was receiving huge amounts of letters to the editor and SMS messages in those early months of 2005 as her plight seemed to reach into every Gold Coast home and the publicity was also growing rapidly across the nation.

On March 16, 2005 the Corby team dropped a 'bombshell' when they announced they had a sworn statement which was 'dynamite' and showed that the 4.1kg (9lbs) of marijuana was planted in her boogie-board bag. Bakir alleged the AFP was aware of the sworn statement and had interviewed its author.

'We have somebody who has told us the times and destinations and the way the bag went through the customs process,' he said. 'We have a statement from a man who has told us Schapelle is not involved and that she is the victim of Australian drug trafficking. He has told us who the people are who are responsible for this, where the drugs are, how they came into this, how the drugs got into her bag, they have named all these people.'

Rasiah said: 'Schapelle should not stay in jail for one minute longer'. He said the man had contacted him on February 1, 2005 with the details of a conversation he had overheard.

'Some time back he overheard some conversation between two guys he knew who were talking about some drugs,' said Rasiah. 'He heard them saying the drugs were put into a bag at Brisbane Airport and were meant to be picked up at Sydney but they must have put them into the wrong bag. They were supposed to go into a particular bag. He heard them say: "Some poor chick has copped it".'

It quickly emerged that the man in question was a Victorian prisoner and the conversation he had overheard was inside a Victorian prison. Although somewhat excited by the news, decades of working as a crime reporter meant I had dealt with my share of prisoners and I knew they would concoct all sorts and weird and wonderful tales if they thought it would help them in some way, so I had some strong, initial reservations.

Schapelle clutched Mercedes' hand through the bars on March 17, 2005 and she said 'Oh my God' when told there was evidence that could save her. 'I can't even talk. I feel numb,' she said with tears streaming down her face and her eyes wide with shock. But she remained cautious about the revelation.

'Of course I'm happy. But I don't want to get my hopes up yet, just in case,' she said from the holding cell at a Denpasar court where her lawyer had successfully requested a week-long adjournment to lodge the new statement. The then Opposition Foreign Affairs spokesman (and now Prime Minister) Kevin Rudd said he had contacted the Indonesian Ambassador in Australia to see if a way could be found for the potential new witness to appear in an Indonesian court.

AFP Commissioner Mick Keelty described the new evidence as 'hearsay' at best. He said the Victorian prisoner's statement contained no direct evidence to Schapelle's case. 'It does mention Corby, but only in the sense that the prisoner made the conclusion that it was connected to Corby's case and overheard other prisoners talking about the Corby case,' he said. 'It's at best hearsay evidence.' Mr Keelty hit out at the decision to publicise what he described as 'spurious allegations', saying it could be counter productive. 'To actually parade all these spurious allegations in the Australian media can be doing Schapelle Corby no good at all,' he said.

The union representing Australian airport baggage handlers, the Transport Workers Union, also weighed into the debate, asking for the allegations to be investigated urgently.

Bakir said the Australian government had a duty to investigate the Victorian prisoner's claims. 'Mr Keelty can say whatever he likes, the fact of the matter is there is a girl in jail who could be executed,' he said.

'They need to take this matter very, very seriously. At this stage, the Australian Government has done nothing to ensure her safety. It is important for the Australian Government and the AFP to investigate this matter.'

Rasiah asked Australians to put pressure on Prime Minister Howard and Foreign Minister Downer to act on the matter. Mr Keelty responded to those comments and said it was not the role of the AFP to give support to lawyers defending Australians jailed around the globe.

But although the court had agreed to hear evidence from Australia, there had not been any direct indication that it would lead to Schapelle's freedom.

11:
The hearings continue

BAKIR and Rasiah met with the then Australian Attorney-General Philip Ruddock and the former Federal Justice and Customs Minister Senator Chris Ellison on March 18, 2005 and during the 90-minute meeting, they requested that the still unidentified Victorian prisoner be sent to Bali to testify at the following week's hearing.

There was naturally a deal of speculation about the identity of the prisoner, why he was in prison and how detailed and accurate was his information about Schapelle and the drugs.

Bakir said he explained to Mr Ruddock and Mr Ellison that 'we needed to have that man available to give evidence in Bali next week as it could be critical to Schapelle's case and we don't have any more chances'.

'He (Ruddock) told us he would see if it could be done. We also asked if AFP officers could also give evidence in Bali next week about drug trafficking between Australian airports because we have evidence that it is very common and there is no security, and we discussed those allegations for a while. He said he would find out if AFP officers could take the stand in Bali.'

A member of Mr Ruddock's staff confirmed the content of the conversation to me and said Mr Ruddock had assured

Schapelle's legal team that the government was doing all it could and would continue to do so. As Bakir and Rasiah continued their round of meetings with government ministers and police officials, the Queensland Police Commissioner Bob Atkinson said on March 21, 2005 that Queensland police were assisting AFP officers to track down and interview a number of prisoners who were allegedly overheard discussing Schapelle's case in a Victorian prison.

'My understanding is that the alleged conversation occurred between a number of prisoners in a Victorian prison and my understanding is that the federal police are endeavouring to interview... at least one other person who has since been released from prison,' he said. He said that person was at one stage in a Queensland prison, but was of Victorian origin. 'At this stage we are assisting... to locate that particular individual but I really can't take it further than that at this stage.'

At Schapelle's next court appearance, on March 24, 2005, she was trembling and crying almost continually, and was told it was her last chance to address officials of the Denpasar District Court. Speaking to the three judges and with Rosleigh and Mercedes watching the proceedings, a shaking Schapelle pleaded with them to let her go home.

'I love my family, I love my dad, I wanted to take a holiday, I don't like drugs and I know there's a big penalty in Indonesia and all over the world,' she said. 'I would never jeopardise my life in this situation and my family's health and everyone who loves me to do something like this.'

She then turned to the three prosecutors and said: 'Please find it in your hearts to get all the facts, all the evidence, use your own heart and your mind... to find it in your heart to maybe bring justice to the right people.'

In a flood of tears, Schapelle said she loved Bali and would never put the justice system 'to the test'. During almost two hours of testimony, she stuck to her story that the drugs were not hers and that someone else had planted them in her bag. 'It is not mine, I did not put it there,' she said, pointing to her boogie-board bag and the stash of marijuana sitting in the court.

Asked by Head Judge Sirait why she did not want to touch her bag and the drugs, she responded: 'This has destroyed my life, why would I want to touch it. I have never been involved in drugs.'

Earlier, senior Qantas baggage handler Scott Speed told the court that the Australian airline had a rule disallowing anything being placed in a boogie-board bag apart from the board itself. He said it was unlikely that the marijuana was in the bag when Schapelle checked it in.

He was asked about the flippers being in the bag and he replied that something small like that could get through but he added that '95 per cent of the staff' would make passengers remove anything sizeable from a boogie-board bag.

Australian criminologist Professor Paul Wilson, from the Gold Coast's Bond University also gave evidence that morning, stating that Schapelle was innocent. He admitted that he had met her for the first time the previous day. 'I can look at her face and talk to people who know her well and honestly say she did not know the drugs were in the bag,' he said. He said she did not fit the profile of a drug trafficker and Schapelle's supporters applauded his words. Professor Wilson has studied a number of drug traffickers in Thailand. Later he told me he was concerned about Schapelle's mental state following his visit to Kerobokan.

'She oscillates between being very down and being strong and determined to go on, but her down times are growing more frequent, which is to be expected given her circumstances,' he said.

'On the night before her court appearance where I testified, she was very depressed and low, but the next morning, by the time she was taken to court, she had pulled herself together. I found her to be very honest, very straightforward. Before I left the Gold Coast, I was not sure of her innocence or otherwise, but now I'm convinced she had no knowledge of those drugs. She is a direct young Australian of average intelligence who has been caught up in a horror story that is not of her doing and she is finding life in that prison very hard.'

Some months later, after some media reference to suicide, Schapelle told me during one of my visits to Kerobokan that she would not consider committing suicide because of what it would do her family and friends. Rosleigh has always been scathing whenever suicide and Schapelle have been mentioned together, saying it would never happen.

On March 25, 2005, Justice and Customs Minister, Senator Chris Ellison approved the transfer of the Victorian remand prisoner who was now identified as John Patrick Ford to give evidence in Bali on March 27, 2005. Ford was awaiting trial at the time on charges of rape, aggravated burglary, threat to kill, unlawful imprisonment and assault. He was escorted by Corrections Victoria staff on a flight that arrived in Bali on the afternoon of March 27, 2005. The Australian Consul General in Bali, Brent Hall, met Ford at the airport before he was transferred into the custody of Balinese authorities.

Ford's ex-wife Rita told the Australian media she was proud of him for offering to testify, but said she was worried about his safety. She said there was no benefit for him travelling to Bali to testify. Schapelle's team was hoping against hope that his evidence would free Schapelle, but I had serious doubts that the evidence of a prisoner in handcuffs would carry much weight with the Indonesian judges. Sadly, I was proved correct.

Remand prisoner Ford, dressed neatly in a shirt and tie and wearing dark trousers, told the specially convened court that he had overheard two other prisoners he identified as Terry and Paul laughing in Victoria's Port Phillip Prison in November 2004 as they discussed how Schapelle had become an innocent drug mule for a jailed drug dealer he named as Ronnie Vigenza.

He said that Terry was a 'player' with underworld connections in Melbourne and Sydney. Ford told the court he was '100 per cent sure' that Vigenza owned the 4.1kg (9lbs) of marijuana. He mentioned another man, a Brisbane baggage handler who he claimed put the drugs into Schapelle's bag, but he refused to name this fourth man saying: 'I am 100 per cent certain that if I mentioned this man's name in relation to these cases, when I get back to Australia, I will be killed,' he said.

'Schapelle Corby is the victim of domestic drug trafficking by what I regard as petty criminals and cowards. They (Terry and Paul) found it very funny that Ronnie's drugs had gone missing, they found it very funny that they had ended up in Indonesia and they were very specific about the amount of drugs and they were very specific about how they were taken. They were quite clear it was supposed to go from Brisbane to Sydney and be delivered in Sydney. It was definitely Corby's bag. All I can say to the court is that there is no way on God's earth that Ms Corby is a drug trafficker. I know better than that. I think the court can see that as well. My belief is so strong I will put my personal safety at risk, and I'm not asking anything in return. I just want to see justice done.'

The then 40-year-old Ford denied to the court he had come forward so he could have a 'holiday' in Bali and said he took 'great personal risk' of his face and identity becoming widely known. He spoke very softly as he gave evidence and a tearful Schapelle at times leant forward to hear him, at other times biting her lip as she listened intently. After two hours of testimony, Ford was taken from the court and returned to Australia. Schapelle's only comment was that she hoped he was telling the truth.

But Ronnie Vigenza certainly didn't think the truth had been told, labelling Ford a 'bloody liar'. The then 38-year-old, living in the northern Melbourne suburb of Reservoir, told *The Herald Sun* on March 29, 2005 that he had nothing to do with any drug ring and that he was trying to get his life back together after getting out of jail six years earlier. While he was being interviewed, Vigenza's wallet contained $4.55 in change, a Medicare card, a pension card and a video store card. 'Have a look around—do I look like a drug lord?' he said. 'I don't know what I could have done to this fella (Ford). He's named me as the man who financed the whole deal and I don't even have a bank account.' He said he had been in jail when Schapelle was arrested.

Vigenza said he recognised Ford from the Port Phillip Prison, where he used to serve the food, but did not know him well. 'I know his face, but if he did not put his face up, I wouldn't have known him as John Ford,' he said. He said he had never spoken to Ford and did not know why he had been named. 'I might have given him one spud less than the others,' he said. He said he would have been happy to help Schapelle if he could, but he had no knowledge of any drugs being planted on her.

Vigenza said he was no 'cleanskin' (a person with no criminal record) but he always owned up when he was in the wrong. 'I've been in court 50 times and I've only pleaded not guilty once,' he said. This whole episode did not help Schapelle's image at home—these guys were all convicted criminals in Australia and Schapelle being associated with them in any way, even just by name, was really quite damaging.

Early in April 2005, Michael senior rushed back to Bali to see

Schapelle for the first time in three months and he was his usual blunt self when he was fronted by the media outside the prison. He told journalist Cindy Wockner that he and Schapelle had tried hard to keep it together. 'It cracks me up to see her like that,' he said. 'I can see that the pressure is getting to her. It's getting down to the nitty-gritty of it now. She was trying hard. She is strong, but me, I'm not. She's not feeling too well at the moment.'

The 'moment' he referred to was only a few days before Schapelle's lawyers expected the prosecutors to ask for the death penalty in their summing up.

In April, Indonesian President Susilo Bambang Yudhoyono visited Australia. It was his first official visit and John Howard told Sydney radio station 2GB that he was careful in raising the issue of Schapelle's case.

'She's still in court and quite properly, if a foreign leader came to Australia and asked me to do something about the outcome of a trial in this country, I would say "Well it's not my place to do that because the courts are independent",' he said. 'We did, however, in discussion have the attorney-general (Philip Ruddock) raise the question of some general issues relating to the operation of the mutual assistance treaty under which that witness (Ford) was sent to Indonesia and also some other related matters. I think that was the appropriate thing to do. I feel for her. I feel for her family, I feel for anybody—guilty or innocent—in a situation like that, obviously far more if they are innocent. We just have to wait and see. But the Indonesian justice system has to be respected, just as we ask other people to respect our justice system.'

The next hearing on April 7, 2005 was postponed by the prosecutors. This came only two days after President Yudhoyono told *The Australian* newspaper that he would be watching the

Corby case 'closely to make sure that justice is there, because justice is important to be upheld and everybody, including the people of Australia and the people of Indonesia, will watch that kind of fairness of justice'.

Members of Schapelle's legal team were in Jakarta that week to meet Australian Justice Minister Chris Ellison. Senator Ellison met with his Indonesian counterpart Hamid Awaludin to discuss a prisoner exchange program between the two nations, one which could eventually be of benefit to Schapelle.

Unlike Australia's British-based legal system where a person is innocent until proven guilty, the reverse is the case in Indonesia, where the law has evolved from the days when the archipelago was a Dutch colony. Rasiah conceded to me that the defence team had not been able to prove who planted the 4.1kg (9lbs) of marijuana in Schapelle's bag.

'As I have said all along, the drugs were found in her bag, she has admitted it was her bag, and that is sufficient for a guilty verdict in this country,' he said.

'But the fact that we have doubt creeping into the prosecution is a very positive thing for Schapelle and they are seeking advice from superiors in Jakarta about whether to accept the evidence of events in Australia with airport baggage handlers and drugs being transported from airport to airport domestically. If the Australian Government can admit that this is the case, and we know it is because the AFP have arrested bag handlers over matters in Sydney, and also say the name Schapelle Corby has not come up in any police investigation into these matters, then I truly believe that Schapelle can walk free. As it is, she has already served six months in jail for having an unlocked bag.'

He said he hoped to persuade Mr Ellison to make a statement about drug transportation in Australia. 'And that sort of a statement does not constitute interference in another country's judicial system but it is simply a statement about the situation in Australia relevant to the case,' he said. 'Then all the Australian evidence presented so far could be taken into account.'

As far as I was concerned, this was Rasiah's finest effort thus far and it seemed that President Yudhoyono's direct reference to Schapelle's case that week may have spooked the prosecution and as we found out, the longer the case went on, Jakarta ruled over the proceedings entirely. It is likely that some of the prosecutors were having some doubts, but a visit to Jakarta seemed to put them back on track, and that was not good for Schapelle.

Mercedes told me that Schapelle had burst into tears when told of the adjournment. 'It's been really hard and scary for her, all this waiting and not knowing, and it's getting really hard for her now,' she said. 'And it's getting to me a bit and my shoulders are drooping a bit now. The support of other Australians is helping her a lot and there are lots of people she has never seen before coming to the jail every day. It's amazing really.'

12:
The trial begins

IT came as no surprise to me when a pasty-looking Schapelle, clutching her stomach, told the Denpasar District Court officials that she was 'really sick'. She had vomited after being led through the usual threatening throng of media pressing in on her outside the court.

Head judge Linton Sirait adjourned the April 7 hearing, telling Schapelle to look after herself.

As well as the stomach bug, family members said her health deterioration was a culmination of just over six months in jail, the weekly pressure of the court and media pack and the fact that the court was nearing its decision, which was now expected to be finalised in late May. Mercedes said a doctor would visit Schapelle and assess her condition. 'It's just everything, stressed, sore stomach, diarrhoea, vomiting,' she told me.

On Monday, April 11, 2005 a person sent a threatening letter to the Indonesian Consulate in Perth. The letter contained live bullets and it demanded Schapelle's release or it warned that someone at the consulate would be killed. This clearly was not at all helpful to Schapelle's case.

Two days before her next scheduled appearance, Ron Bakir proposed through the media a $1 million reward for the person who could prove Schapelle innocent. He said he would donate $100,000 towards the reward and implored Australian businesses to back him. 'I want 900 businesses or concerned citizens to donate $1000 each and the $1 million will be paid to anyone who can absolutely prove that Schapelle is innocent of this alleged crime,' he told me by mobile phone as he was en route back to Bali.

'I hope people can come forward with this money to one of my Mad Ron stores as quickly as possible but I'm confident we will raise the necessary amount. If anyone can help Schapelle, then one million bucks will be up for grabs.'

Queensland Opposition Leader Lawrence Springborg called on the then Queensland Premier Peter Beattie to contribute $100,000, saying the Premier had been quiet on the subject 'despite the prospect of a Queensland girl facing the firing squad'.

The next court appearance on April 14, 2005 was the most dramatic thus far, with Schapelle collapsing in court amid scenes of hysteria and chaos. When she arrived at the courthouse, she was handcuffed to a female Indonesian prisoner and the media pack was all over them. The other woman fainted in the crush, dragging Schapelle down with her and she passed out as well.

Mercedes raced in, screaming at the media to leave her sister alone and swung her handbag, hitting an Indonesian journalist across the head. After court, Mercedes told me by phone that the two handcuffed woman were being pushed and intimidated by the media scrum.

'She has always hated that walk into court and she could barely breathe today (April 14, 2005) and then they both fainted,' she said. 'They both hit the deck and the Indonesian press guys were just trampling the poor Indonesian girl and that's when I waded in swinging and I think I was screaming at them to leave her alone. The police officers had to take the cuffs off and carry Schapelle into court and the other girl was carried in as well.

'It was just crazy and they (the media pack) wouldn't back off. The other girl's wrist was cut from the handcuff and all the pushing on the ground. Inside it was worse. You couldn't breathe and I thought I was going down as well. The Indonesian press were crowding around Schapelle and she sat there and then she just went hysterical and started screaming then she fainted again and I jumped the rail. I hope it didn't look too bad on TV. I hardly know what's happening at the moment. I've just about had it and mum and dad are not good either, especially after this.'

Schapelle fainted again in the witness chair just before the prosecutors were about to announce what penalty they would recommend. She clutched her stomach and fell forward. A huge media pack surged forward and surrounded her, leaving little air to breath. Local doctor Connie Panglahila, asked to be at the court by Australian Consul-General Brent Hall because of fears about her health, treated Schapelle on a courtroom bench as family, media, police, judges and court officials looked on.

Dr Panglahila said Schapelle was suffering from high blood pressure and a lack of oxygen. Mercedes said at this stage, Schapelle's eyes were rolling back in her head as she lay on the wooden bench. With everyone shouting and the court in uproar, the judges ordered Schapelle back to her cell for a medical check up.

While all this was happening, Mick jumped to his feet and screamed at the media pack to move back from his daughter. 'Come on, you've had enough. You've earned your bread and butter, now on your bike and piss off,' he yelled. 'Let her out of the joint.' It was the most animated he had been at any of the hearings.

It was rare for Mick to shout at that stage, because his hearing was still reasonable and it was also unusual for Rosleigh to cry. It showed how the whole case was getting to the family and when Mercedes recounted that day in court to me, you could hear the stress in her voice.

A weeping Rosleigh asked the crowd to back off so that Schapelle could breathe. Judge Sirait warned Schapelle against play acting, telling her to sit quietly. 'Don't make it up, if you make it up, we will force the court to go on,' he said. Rasiah asked the Balinese police for protection for Schapelle at future court hearings.

At the same time the *Daily Telegraph* in Sydney reported that it had information the prosecutors and Schapelle's legal team had met in Denpasar the previous week to discuss how Schapelle could dodge a firing squad and then serve any future jail term in Australia. All these claims were furiously denied by the prosecutors in Bali and later Bakir told the *Daily Telegraph* that: 'We had normal discussions with them and they said our evidence was not strong enough. I am not going to clear it up any further.'

Rasiah also commented: 'We have serious concerns about reports in sections of the media in Australia that members of our defence team have met with prosecutors to map out some type of a deal,' he said. 'These claims are absolutely false and I can categorically state that no-one from Bali Law Chambers whose team is defending Schapelle Corby had any meetings with any prosecutors in this case. They don't even smile or speak to us in court, let alone hold clandestine meetings with us. Those fabricated stories have caused us a great deal of problems here in Bali and these kind of allegations could be very dangerous for this case.'

On April 17, 2005, the issue of Australians arrested in Indonesia was again in the headlines, but this time it was nine young Australians arrested in Bali over a plan to smuggle 8.3kg (18lbs) of heroin worth $8 million from Bali to Australia. Some of the group were arrested at the airport with the heroin strapped around their waists.

Mick Keelty and the AFP were immediately under criticism in Australia because it was revealed that the AFP had been monitoring the group's movements with the Balinese police and could easily have arrested most of the group when they landed back in Australia where the charge did not carry a death penalty as it did in Indonesia.

The nine Australians—Andrew Chan, Si Yi Chen, Michael Czugaj, Renae Lawrence, Tach Duc Thanh Nguyen, Matthew Norman, Scott Rush, Martin Stephens and Myuran Sukumaran— were all over the TV and newspapers while they were held at Polda. Mercedes and Rosleigh told me that Schapelle planned to have little to do with this group and to a degree she had done just that ever since they arrived at Kerobokan.

On the same day, April 17, 2005, I was tipped off that the prosecutors would be seeking a life sentence for Schapelle. My source also told me that prosecutor Ida Bagus Wiswantanu would ignore all the evidence given by prisoner Ford and consider only the 4.1kg (9lbs) of marijuana found in Schapelle's bag and the fact she had admitted the bag was hers.

Rasiah told me he expected something similar as well. The day before her next court appearance, the *Gold Coast Bulletin* Voteline, which had asked readers if they believed Schapelle was innocent or not, showed a resounding 88 per cent thought she was innocent. It was the same percentage as a poll conducted by Channel 9's A Current Affair the previous week.

On April 19, 2005, prison officers took Schapelle to Sanglah public hospital for a three-hour physical examination, with doctors declaring she was in good health.

At the hearing on April 21, 2005, the prosecutors asked for a life sentence. Despite having taken a tranquillizer, Schapelle sobbed and shook and said: 'My life is over' as her interpreter told her the sombre news. Beginning just after midday, as was often the case, the session left Schapelle shaky on her feet, and she was escorted by 10 police officers through the menacing media scrum.

The court heard chief prosecutor Ida Bagus Wiswantanu ask the three judges to find Schapelle 'officially and convincingly guilty'.

'The defendant's actions can ruin the image of Bali as a tourist destination and her actions can make Bali look like a drug haven and affect young people's lives,' he said. Wiswantanu told the court there were enough drugs in Schapelle's bag for 4200 people, which seemed somewhat fanciful. He said he had not asked for the death penalty because Schapelle had been polite and she did not have any prior convictions. As well as asking for a life sentence, he also asked the court to fine Schapelle 100 million rupiah, which was then worth about $A13,300.

Watched by about 30 Aussie tourists, many dressed more for the beach rather than a court of law, the three prosecutors took turns reading their recommendations during the two-hour hearing. They repeatedly attacked the defence case and witnesses and Wiswantanu was scathing about prisoner John Ford. 'Looking at his background as a prisoner, the reason for him to testify before an Indonesian court was to inhale the air of freedom,' he said. He said Bond University Professor Paul Wilson's judgement of Schapelle did not stem from accurate research.

Qantas baggage handler Scott Speed had explained that baggage leaving Brisbane domestic airport was not X-rayed, paving the way for the drugs to have been in Schapelle's bag when she checked it in, he said.

The evidence of James Corby and the other two travelling mates was not given 'to find truth and justice' as the law dictates, according to the prosecutors, who delivered their summaries in a monotone, impossible to understand unless you were a native Indonesian or fluent in the language.

Schapelle's lawyer Lily Lubis cried during the proceedings, saying later that the prosecutors were 'very unfair'.

After the prosecution's summary ended, a tearful Schapelle went to the barrier and hugged an equally teary Mercedes, telling her: 'It's not fair.' Mercedes tried in vain to comfort her, saying 'It's okay, it's okay,' over and over again.

Guards finally led Schapelle away and a long piercing scream could be heard from the holding cell. Now it was up to the defence team to try to sway the judges with their closing argument the following week.

Schapelle's cousin, Melissa Younger, who had flown in from Perth to lend her support, held Schapelle's hand through the cell bars, then stroked her tear streaked face. She told reporters that she had thought the trial would be fair. 'But I don't think it was, but we will see what the judges say. I told her to be strong and that I love her,' she said.

Rosleigh said the family had been prepared to hear bad news. 'I don't know what to think,' she said. 'I know it's not the end. Our lawyers will be fighting to bring the sentence down anyway. Today is over and she was very, very strong.'

Mick Corby said the news had devastated the family. 'It's terrible thing to hear when it's your daughter,' he told me. 'This is just so hard to understand when you know in your heart that Schapelle is truly innocent. I want to thank the vast majority of Australians for their support and I ask them to keep supporting her through this time.'

By this late stage of the trial in April 2005, everyone in Australia had an opinion about Schapelle and her family. The media was all over the story and rumours were rife about family members and whether or not they were involved in drug dealing. It was then looking like another trial by media scenario that Lindy Chamberlain-Creighton went through. On the evening of August 17, 1980, Lindy Chamberlain and her husband Michael were camping at Uluru with their three children—Aidan, then 6, Reagan who was four at the time and Azaria who was nine weeks and four days old.

Azaria vanished from the tent, there was blood inside the tent and the famous words uttered by Lindy—'a dingo's got my baby' cannoned around the country and the world. Azaria was never found, but an inquest later confirmed a dingo had killed Azaria. This finding was overturned and Lindy was charged with her child's murder. She spent the next seven years living a nightmare —with three of them in prison—before she proved her innocence and received a complete exoneration—which was a first for the Australian legal system.

The Chamberlain case divided the nation and everyone had an opinion on Lindy's guilt or innocence. Schapelle's case is probably bigger than the Chamberlain one, certainly in terms of media. There was no internet when Lindy was front page news and it's unlikely that live TV and nightly television updates would have been as easy 25 years ago as they have been in this case.

Schapelle was only five years old when 34-year-old Lindy was sentenced to life with hard labour and knew little of what had happened in the Chamberlain case. But both women became media obsessions and both have endured wild rumours, sick jokes and truckloads of speculation. Jail changed Lindy Chamberlain-Creighton as it already has with Schapelle. Lindy

Chamberlain-Creighton made contact with Schapelle by letter to the prison in mid-2005, telling her what had happened to Schapelle 'made me feel like I had been kicked all over again. My heart bleeds for you.' For Lindy the whole thing finally dried up, but for Schapelle that hasn't happened yet and in 2005 the rumours and media circus were just ramping up.

Professor Paul Wilson, chair of Criminology and Forensic Psychologist at Bond University on the Gold Coast, met Schapelle in Kerobokan and gave defence evidence for her in 2005. He believes Schapelle was newsworthy because she is attractive, was vulnerable on holiday in a foreign land, and was adamant and unbending about her innocence.

'These characteristics are very common among other women who have been the centre of media attention over high profile crimes (Lindy Chamberlain, Joanne Lees and the Falconio case, Jean Lee the first woman hanged in Australia),' he said.

'All these women were attractive and rebellious and, although two of them were not in a foreign land, they were on holiday and away from their homes. I doubt very much that a male, or an older, less physically attractive woman would have received anywhere near the same sort of media attention.'

Mick Corby was angry about the rumours which were circulating in Australia about Schapelle and her family. 'As for all those rumours about members of the Corby family being drug dealers, well it's all crap, we are just an ordinary family and we don't have anything to do with drugs and we don't have much money at all,' he said.

'I heard listeners on radio asking how Schapelle could afford to go to Bali all the time. Well, it was her first trip for years and she saved up for it for ages. Then they were asking why she took a body board to Bali when Mercedes and Wayan own a surf shop in Bali. They don't live in Bali, they live in Australia. And they don't own any surf business anywhere—that's total crap as well.'

News also surfaced at this time that claimed Schapelle's legal team had rejected an offer of help from two of Australia's top criminal QCs. The two Perth silks, Mark Trowell, QC and Tom Percy, QC, said they had tried countless times to approach Schapelle's legal team, only to be met with a wall of silence. I had a handful of telephone conversations with Mr Trowell, including three lengthy ones, and I have no doubt their vast and special experience would have been a great help to Schapelle, particularly during the appeal stage. Mr Trowell told me that he was approached by Australian Attorney-General Phillip Ruddock at a law conference in Brisbane in March and asked if he would be prepared to help Schapelle's legal team.

'We are prepared to do this pro bono and we are certainly not looking at it as a profile building exercise, because neither of us needs that,' he told me by phone. 'We just felt we have the expertise to help someone in trouble in another country and from what we have seen, she (Schapelle) could certainly do with some help.'

Mr Trowell, who has top level contacts in Indonesian legal and government circles, said he had called two different partners at Tampoe's law firm in Surfers Paradise, Hoolihans, but there had not been any return calls. Tampoe claimed he and his partners never received any phone messages at his office.

All over the nation, Australians were watching Schapelle's life unfold on TV and in newspapers and magazines like a frightening soap opera. At this stage opinions were very highly in favour of Schapelle and some supporters were even calling for the return of the aid monies the Australian Government gave to Indonesia after the Boxing Day tsunami the previous year.

Schapelle's case was now leading all TV news broadcasts

and was almost daily front-page news across the country. Even the Oscar winning Australian actor Russell Crowe joined the burgeoning pro-Schapelle bandwagon when on April 22, 2005, he appealed to the Australian Government to act to save her, in a public statement saying the charges against her were questionable.

'When there is such doubt, how can we, as a country, stand by and let a young lady, as an Australian, rot away in a foreign prison,' he told the John Laws radio program. 'That is ridiculous. We just gave Indonesia how many hundreds of millions of dollars in tsunami relief. We're not disrespecting your (Indonesian) laws or anything, but in our minds, we think there is massive doubt here.'

He said Schapelle should be returned to Australia to face trial under our judicial system. 'The photograph of Schapelle Corby broke my heart,' said Crowe, referring to front page photos of Schapelle after she had learnt the prosecutors were seeking life imprisonment.

As the defence team prepared for its final submission, Schapelle was writing her own notes in her prison cell, planning to make a final plea to the judges from her heart. Her brother Michael told me Schapelle was 'still putting on a brave face'.

'She knows she has to keep fighting, but inside it must be really hard for her, and that jail is such a terrible place. It really is a shithouse,' he told me on Anzac Day 2005.

On the eve of her next court appearance came another unlikely rumour published in the *Sunday Mail* in Brisbane which mentioned that talkback radio jockeys were speculating that Schapelle was pregnant. Rosleigh said in the *Sunday Mail*. 'People are saying she is pregnant, she is holding her tummy. Anyone who has had diarrhoea and cramps, knows they will get sore stomach muscles. How would you get pregnant in there?'

The prison doctor carried out a pregnancy test on Schapelle on April 26, 2005 and surprise, surprise... it was negative. At least that was one rumour firmly kicked into touch.

13:
The plea of innocence

WITH her last chance to push her case and address the judges, Schapelle Corby turned to face her three impassive judges and with a voice quaking with emotion she told them her life was in their hands, but urged them to put it into their hearts. It was another emotion-charged court appearance and Schapelle's final chance to speak in her defence.

With the court festooned in yellow ribbon by her brother-in-law, Wayan, and with her family and supporters wearing yellow ribbons on their wrists, Schapelle shakily read her handwritten notes, compiled during the previous week in the daylight hours in her cell.

'Firstly, I would like to say to the prosecutors I cannot admit to a crime I did not commit,' she said. 'And to the judges, my life at the moment is in your hands, but I would prefer it in your hearts. And I say again, that I have no knowledge of how the marijuana came to be in my bag. And I believe the evidence shows. One, there is a problem in Australia with security at airports and baggage-handling procedures. Two, my only mistake was not putting a lock on my luggage. Three, I have never at any stage claimed ownership of the plastic bag and its contents. Four, had the police weighed all my luggage for the total weight it would have proven to show a difference from the total weight checked in at Brisbane Airport. The police had the opportunity to fingerprint both plastic bags to prove my innocence, but they chose not to. I am the innocent victim of a tactless drug smuggling network. (For some reason Schapelle then jumps from point four to seven). Seven, I am not a person involved in drugs and I'm not a person who might become involved in a drug smuggling operation. Eight, I love Bali and I would never want to create problems for any of its people. Nine, I believe the seven months which I've already been in prison is severe enough punishment for not putting locks on my bags. My heart and my family are painfully burdened by all these accusations and rumours about me and I don't know how long I can survive in here. I swear that as God is my witness, I did not know that the marijuana was in my bag. Please look to your God for guidance in your judgement of me, for God only speaks for justice. And your honours, I ask for you to show compassion, to find me innocent, to send me home. *Saya tidak bersalah*. (I am not guilty).'

Her supporters applauded her and then she approached the bench and handed the judges a copy of her speech. Schapelle's handwritten notes were in English. It is doubtful that the judges understood much of what she said and you could not glean anything from studying their faces during her speech. Judge Sirait said he would get her statement translated, which the judges were given the next day.

While Schapelle made her emotional plea, the media was at its feral best outside the courthouse, with TV crews exchanging blows and photographers hitting the dusty ground as they jostled one another for the best positions. One snapper was even slammed into a tree.

Schapelle's lawyers Lily Lubis and Erwin Siregar spent the best part of an hour reading from a 75-page submission fancifully titled 'Does Justice Still Exist for a Defendant in this Beloved Country'. They said the drugs were placed in Schapelle's bag at Brisbane Airport after she checked it in, saying it was a 'public secret' that Australian domestic airports were used by drug syndicates to transfer their illegal stashes across the country using travellers' unlocked baggage. Lubis and Siregar attacked the Balinese Customs officers, finally making the point that three of the four involved with Schapelle spoke no English and the fourth had only scant knowledge of the language, leading to a twisted, inaccurate summation of what happened with Schapelle's boogie-board bag.

The two lawyers attacked Customs officers and police for failing to weigh all the baggage together to make a comparison with Australian records and they also lambasted the police for failing to fingerprint the two plastic bags containing the marijuana, especially the inner bag. And they referred to the fact that the marijuana was worth a great deal more in Australia than Bali. They also had a shot at the prosecutors for claiming the marijuana was top grade, despite refusing the defence's desperate plea to have it tested.

Siregar described the prosecutors as 'street magicians who can pull a rabbit from a hat without knowing where the rabbit came from'.

Erwin Siregar, who was not a member of Bali Law Chambers, put in a solid effort.

Mercedes later told me that Schapelle had been okay in court that day. 'But it's the time all this is taking that is wearing her down so much,' she said. 'Normally she is sort of frozen after court, but today I could talk to her, so I knew it was better than the last few weeks.' The time factor was something Mercedes mentioned often in mid-2005. That same day, Mick Corby told the ABC's *7.30 Report* that there was no sign of drugs when she packed the boogie-board before she left for Bali. He said she had not touched drugs since her school days. 'She had nothing to do with bloody drugs,' he said. 'Oh, she might have had a pull when she was in bloody Grade 10 or something, around the back of the schoolyard like kids do. I don't know. She had nothing to do with it since, or any time as far as I know. Anyway, I'd have seen the bloody bag there. There was nothing in it. They (the drugs) turned up over there somewhere between Brisbane Airport and Bali. I couldn't tell you where.'

This grilling of Michael Corby was the public beginning of the media turning their powerful spotlight onto the rest of the family. To varying degrees the whole family has been on trial by media ever since. This was no longer just about Schapelle and the contents of her boogie-board bag, this was digging into whatever she had done in her past life as well as her family being put through the media wringer. Naturally this had nothing to do with Schapelle receiving a fair trial or her appeals, but it made great viewing or reading as far as the Australian and Indonesian media were concerned and they were not about to let it go.

In Bali, only 24 hours after Schapelle's emotional submission, Head Judge Sirait said her words carried no legal weight and he would basically ignore them. 'Not enough. He or she has to prove he or she is not guilty,' he said. 'Every inmate would say I'm not guilty. I'm still looking for something related to the law.' Before uttering these portentous words, Judge Sirait had sentenced a South African man found guilty of heroin offences to life imprisonment.

Back home on the Gold Coast a 'real low life' stole a Schapelle Corby collection box from the counter of her mother's fish and chip shop in the working class suburb of Southport on April 29, 2005. Rosleigh said the box was nearly full and would have contained between $150 and $200, mainly in coins. 'We get a lot of pensioners in the shop and they say things like 'It's pension day tomorrow, so we can spare 50c for Schapelle,' she said. 'It was pretty busy and I was serving this fellow and the collection box was on the counter when I started serving him and when I turned around again it was gone and it's amazing no-one noticed someone taking it. It's pretty devastating to think someone would do that to these pensioners and Schapelle, but the person who did this will get paid back somehow, they always do.'

Rosleigh said the whole exercise of looking after Schapelle in jail, paying her growing legal fees and the family's airfares was a serious and constant drain on family finances.

'I used the money from the collection box to buy clothes for Schapelle and I have had to buy quite a bit because she keeps losing weight and her clothes don't fit any more—plus I buy her soap and shampoo and other little things like that.'

It must be remembered that there is not even drinking water available for free in Kerobokan prison. The prisoner can buy bottled water inside the prison or someone has to supply it and with the perpetually humid and hot Balinese climate, Schapelle consumes several standard-size bottles daily. Sometimes she even uses it to wash her face as the available water can give you skin diseases.

Rosleigh had struggled to keep the Rox fish shop going in Scarborough Street because she had spent so much time in Bali, but she had been helped by her son Michael and some of Schapelle's friends.

Early on, the media kept referring to her 'media deal' but in reality it was a strange set up. Channel 9's *A Current Affair* had talked her into signing a contract that they would pay for Ros's airfares and accommodation in Bali in return for her exclusive interviews. I never had a problem talking with her for my reports and if something came up and she wanted to talk to other media, then she did. She is not person who can easily be gagged, as some Channel 9 staffers discovered. *A Current Affair* did well out of the deal because she always stayed at budget accommodation in Bali, even though the wording of the contract would allow her luxury digs. The contract is valid until seven days after Schapelle is freed. Ros has been told it would be easy to have it voided but she hasn't bothered and she is now paying her own airfares and staying at Mercedes and Wayan's home.

The prosecutors were almost cocky when they summed up their case on May 6, 2005, saying they had presented enough damning evidence to have Schapelle locked away for life. And in a disturbing sign, the three judges appeared to nod in agreement as the prosecutors delivered their final statement to the court. They said Schapelle's legal team had tried to win over the judges with a wave of emotion rather than facts. They said that it was a legal fact that Schapelle had brought the drugs to Bali in her unlocked bag and that the defence witness statements from family and friends of Schapelle could not be trusted.

Earlier in that week, Victorian prisoner John Ford had been stabbed in prison and Mercedes said she and Schapelle had been unaware of it until media members yelled it out to them as they came into court. 'Schapelle was pretty shocked, but he had said he feared for his life and he was right about that, that poor man. He should not have been in a situation where he could be attacked,' she told me. 'But he also said he feared for Schapelle's life and I'm sure that will now be preying on her mind a lot. I just hope she's safe here.'

Then, on May 11, I and one or two journalists uncovered an amazing 'coincidence'. I was looking at some AAP copy on the internet news stream about a drug-smuggling ring operating through Sydney Airport when I noticed the date and it literally caused me to shake. It had turned out that while Schapelle and her unlocked boogie-board bag were at Sydney Airport on October 8, 2004, baggage handlers were smuggling 9.9kg (22lbs) of cocaine off a flight from South America and that they had been paid $300,000 to get the briefcase containing the drug through the airport.

The coincidence of the date came to light when documents were tendered in Sydney's Central Local Court during a failed bail application for one of the 12 men charged with importing $15 million worth of cocaine.

After seeing the report, I contacted the court in Sydney to confirm the date was accurate, then I rang Mercedes in Bali. She was stunned and there was silence on the line for a moment. 'It's really spooky that on the same day there were kilograms of illicit drugs floating around that airport that we now know of,' she said.

'That cannot be a coincidence and more and more it all points to what the defence has been saying about my innocent sister. I try not to get too excited, but this is just amazing news and surely it must help free Schapelle, although I know we may have to wait for an appeal now and I'm trying to prepare Schapelle that she will have to be strong for a longer time yet.'

I later told Mercedes that in all my years as a police reporter, I knew of many good police investigators in Australia and England who all said the same thing: 'I do not believe in coincidence where a crime has been committed.'

Mercedes made an impassioned plea on behalf of the Corby family for the Howard Government to use all its influence to have her sister freed immediately. 'This latest, startling information revealed in the Sydney court should be enough for the Prime Minister to intervene, as it is now clear there is a serious travesty of justice here, as we have always said. I think it would be unfair if Schapelle has to remain in the burrowing hell hole for further months waiting for an appeal to something that clearly should not be in court.'

But Australia Federal Police Commissioner Mick Keelty said that if called to give evidence in Schapelle's Bali trial, he could not fully support the theory.

'There is little intelligence to suggest that baggage handlers are using innocent people to traffic heroin or other drugs between states,' he said. 'We can only go by the intelligence we've got. If I was to give evidence in a case like Corby's, I would have to be honest and I would have to say that's what the intelligence produces.'

Obviously, it is two different drug rings, but it raises the questions of a lucrative business running at Sydney Airport. The revelations also should have strengthened the suspicion that there was a drug-trafficking ring transporting drugs between Brisbane and Sydney airports.

Some AFP personnel could have known about the same date scenario and realised its potential significance to Schapelle's case, which had been in Australian media for months, and others could have known of the cocaine bust itself at Sydney Airport the day Schapelle was arrested in Bali. Yet through all the debate about Australian airport security that had been on the table since October 2004, no-one from the AFP publicly raised the cocaine bust at all.

The cocaine bust at Sydney Airport prompted the then Qantas Chief Executive Geoff Dixon to comment. 'I can't rule out any link,' he said. 'All I can say is that we have looked very carefully over the past five months and we've known what's been going on and we haven't found any connections, but I can't say anything more than that.'

Mr Dixon's comments, plus the cocaine bust, came to light

after Schapelle's case was effectively closed, with only rebuttal and the verdict to follow.

While all these issues relating to the case were being aired through the media daily, by May 2005 the Schapelle Corby sideshow, complete with merchandising, was also in full swing. If you Googled the name Schapelle Corby in mid 2005, there were some 254,000 entries and even in 2008, there are still more than 200,000—quite amazing for someone only known in her immediate circle on October 7, 2004.

As support for Schapelle ballooned to its zenith in May 2005, the *Gold Coast Bulletin* was publishing full pages of SMS messages and emails, all supporting their fellow Gold Coaster.

Hobart travel agent Tony Foster made national news when he said if Schapelle was found guilty, he would never send another client to Bali. He received almost 200 phone calls or emails of support for his stance. On the internet, there were 15 sites relating to Schapelle and at one stage two domain names were for sale on e-Bay. The woman involved in this told me that she had been offered $150,000 for one of the domain names by a clothing company.

Melbourne singer Jason Stan penned 'Song for Schapelle' which was available on CD online and a Sydney man tried to copyright the name Schapelle Corby in May 2005, so he could create books and movies about her. A film crew led by Sydney documentary maker Janine Hosking was to spend about three years filming, shadowing the Corbys everywhere in Bali. They ended up with hundreds of hours in the can and finally released a movie-length doco in the American cinema circuit with the unfortunate title *Ganga Queen*.

This documentary was released in Australia in early July 2008, throwing more opinion against the Corby family. A shorter version of the same documentary was released on the HBO channel in Canada and the United States during the same month and its airing gained a Schapelle a legion of new supporters. There were even reports of Americans cancelling their Balinese holidays in protest.

In 2005, there were people selling 'Free Schapelle' t-shirts, caps, fridge magnets, bumper stickers, stubby holders, paint, chicken stock, dried fruit and vegetables, varnishes, clocks, mouse pads, clothing, and one Queensland guy was even selling sexy 'Free Schapelle' lingerie. An American-based street fashion label, FreshJive released a t-shirt, with the mis-spelt slogan on the front reading 'Free Shapelle Corby' but in smaller print underneath were the words: 'Coz I need my weed back'.

By far the tackiest commercialisation example emerged in 2006 called 'Schapelle Corby Tours'. It claimed to be operated by a man named Eddie Hutauruk, complete with a man's picture. The website said he had been running tours in Bali for eight years and Corby Tours was their latest venture. It had totally disgusting tour claims such as: 'Feeding Time (starts at 12 noon)—Watch Schapelle being fed at either lunch or dinner. Optional extra: for $A10 you can feed Schapelle yourself—watch her face light up as you throw pieces of food to her'. There was a Denpasar address on the website, but it led nowhere when Mercedes and Wayan checked it out.

At least three people or groups have tried to trademark Schapelle's name. Rosleigh finally retained a Sydney lawyer to sort that one out. Some of the internet sites encouraged people to send money in support. I know that some of these sites would have had large sums of money, running into tens of thousands of dollars at least, donated in the month of May, especially towards the end around verdict day, by caring Australians who believed the money would go to the Corby family.

I also talked to media guru Harry M Miller who told me that

Schapelle and her family needed a set up like his organisation to help her. I wholeheartedly agreed with him and I raised the issue with the Corbys.

Schapelle told me she could not understand or believe that people could just take and use her name for profit or to boost their own profiles.

'I just can't believe they can steal and use my name—it's mine,' she told me, shaking her head. Her dad, Mick, said people making money off Schapelle were nothing more than 'vultures and parasites'. He said the entire family had been 'astounded and then angered' by the plethora of 'low opportunists' making money out of Schapelle.

'They are just as bad as looters and it makes me sick that they are doing this, using Schapelle's name,' he told me at his Tugun home. 'She is sitting in a stinking jail and people are making money out of her name, or taking cheap shots at her in so-called satirical websites that are not funny at all. There is nothing funny about this situation.

'These people have no principles or morals. We don't know anything about these websites except we are not getting any money out of it at all and we could really use some money because all this is costing a lot of money for us.

'And some of the things they have said on some of these websites—they just make me sick and I don't look at them anymore. I wish there was some way to stop it.'

14:
The build up to verdict day

SIX days before the verdict, the *Weekend Australian* hit the streets with a front page stating: 'Meet the Corbys'.

It was easily the most negative article published about the Corbys anywhere thus far. It said that Mick Corby had been busted with drugs at a similar age to Schapelle. It quoted him as saying he was fined $400 for about 2g (0.07oz) of marijuana which wasn't his. 'Some girl had it and they busted the whole joint and I had to go along for the ride,' he told the *Weekend Australian*. He told me he was on crutches with a broken ankle and had been at a party where there was dope and it was raided by police. Some of the partygoers ran, but he couldn't and he was arrested. This happened in the 1970s during the reign of right wing Queensland Premier Joh Bjelke-Petersen. A hallmark of his policies was a heavy-handed police force, who became known for their aggressive arrest tactics.

In 2005, Mick went to Roma Street police headquarters in Brisbane and was able to get a copy of the charge and fine and there was no conviction recorded against him. His children were unaware of the incident as they were not even born when it happened and he had never told them about it. So while *The Australian* had dug up some of his past, they were wrong about his 'drug record'.

The article also linked Schapelle's arrest in Bali with her half brother Clinton's charges. Clinton served an 18-month sentence in Woodford prison, north of Brisbane on 62 charges, including burglary, stealing and unlawful use of motor vehicles. He was released in October 2005. Clint was convicted on a string of charges including break and enter, stealing, fraud and unlawful use of a motor vehicle and he had received a 12-month sentence in August, 2004. When Schapelle was arrested he was serving his sentence in the Woodford Correction Centre, north of Brisbane. He had also been in jail in 2001. Family members described him as the black sheep of the family and he had stolen from most of them at some time. Rosleigh told me that it was so bad at one stage that if Clint was in the house and she needed to go to the toilet, she would take her handbag with her.

After his release, Clint told his mum he was going to do the right thing and he got a job and cleaned his act up.

This was the most damning report about the Corbys thus far because it was *The Australian*—with its reputation as Australia's only national paper—and it was on the streets less than a week before Schapelle's verdict. It contained no new evidence about Schapelle, but it gave her family a bad image that was to grow after the verdict. It was picked up by the media in Indonesia—whether it had any influence on the judges is difficult to gauge.

Naturally, the media in Australia were only reporting in the manner they were because the trial was taking place offshore. If Schapelle had appeared in an Australian court, the media response would have been far more restrained because of the laws.

On Wednesday, May 25, 2005, I flew to Bali with Mick Corby and Kay Danes. I had spoken to Kay by phone but we had never met, although I knew her story. Kay and her husband Kerry had been wrongfully and illegally imprisoned for almost 11 months in Laos in 2000 and Kerry had even been tortured during that time. Kay had decided after being freed to help other Australians imprisoned in foreign countries and had formed an international prisoner advocacy group. It was through this role that she had come into contact with Mercedes and she was going to Bali to talk to Schapelle about her own experience in an Asian jail and offer support.

We were all fairly sombre at Brisbane International Airport and I felt that Kay was unsure of me as she had experienced some unpleasant dealings with unscrupulous journos during her captivity and beyond. Mick, with his hair and beard neatly cut short, and loaded up with his medication for his cancer, was also quiet, naturally pondering what fate awaited his daughter and still smarting over the *Weekend Australian* article.

The flight was mostly uneventful, except for a female ABC reporter who recognised Mick and tried to talk him into doing an interview. Kay, who had worked in security in Asia, was immediately protective and on her guard and she spent most of the flight sitting beside Mick. At one point, she said she was going to the toilet and she asked me to watch Mick and keep the ABC reporter at bay. I did not feel comfortable doing this and just spoke to the young woman who was very pleasant and not as pushy as some. Little did I know how soon my attitude to other media was going to change so dramatically.

When we arrived at the airport in Bali there was a huge crowd of press and camera operators mobbing around Mick. When asked how his health was, he replied: 'It's going downhill thanks to you lot.' The family told me how they were mobbed every time they went to the prison and how they were followed by 'scouts' on motorbikes, forcing them to drive around in circles to lose them.

The Corby family was staying at a 'secret location' in the heart of Kuta—the Kuta Puri Bungalows in Poppy's Lane 1, which seemed a ridiculous choice, but initially it worked well because it was so central to the main tourist area that no-one would think of it as a 'hideaway'. It was here that I met Mercedes for the first time after countless phone conversations and I booked into a room near the family.

The super dope idea

The theory about importing super dope from Australia to Bali arose in small sections of the Australian media in 2005 and although not widely supported or followed, it lingers still in 2008. There is no real logic to this idea and in the three years since it was first suggested, no-one has come forward who has smoked it in Bali or even been offered it. There is no hydroponic marijuana grown in Indonesia and that seems to be the only basis for the theory.

Many commentators and Schapelle and her sister had agonised over and tried to work out just who had placed the marijuana in Schapelle's boogie bag. Was it someone trying to import it into Bali or someone transporting it from Brisbane to Sydney? But while it is well known that marijuana is freely available in Bali, what would be the benefit of taking 'coals to Newcastle.'

There had been some reports in the Australian media about some 'super dope' or 'Aussie Gold'—hydroponic cannabis grown in Australia and smuggled to Bali to be sold to expats and foreigners for top prices. It had been suggested that Schapelle might have been part of this set up. The drugs found in Schapelle's bag have never been tested but on a visual analysis it could be possible that it was hydroponic cannabis. I decided to find out about the so-called super dope so after 11pm, I headed into the dark *jalan kecil* (back streets) of Kuta where I knew the dealers would find me.

I was approached several times by men, stepping out of the shadows, who offered me everything from marijuana to *shabu shabu* (methamphetamine or ice) and heroin. Many of these vanished, but five of those dealers agreed to talk to me. All of them told me they had never heard of hydroponically grown Australian marijuana with its trademark big seed heads being smuggled into Bali.

'That's bull, man. If that type of weed was on the market, then we'd know about it,' said one dealer. 'People like our ganja 'cause it's cheap. It's all part of the Bali trip—cheap T-shirts, cheaper Bintang (local beer) and cheap dope. If people want a bigger hit, then they just buy more, there's plenty to go 'round.'

Another street dealer said it would be very hard to guarantee a regular supply of the so-called 'super dope' from Australia. 'This is not practical because it would be too dangerous to ship in kilos of the stuff and you need that on a regular run to make it worthwhile,' he said. 'It's no good having it for your clients for a week and then not seeing it again for months. That's crazy, man.' The dealers told me that marijuana was worth about $A1100 a kilo in Bali at that time. All the dealers I spoke to said they had not previously heard of Schapelle Corby or her sister Mercedes. 'We have talked among ourselves since Corby was arrested, and we don't know them,' said a third dealer.

I also spoke to a number of expats and foreigners who had lived in Bali for lengthy periods and they also doubted the 'super dope' theory. 'You would have to bring in heaps to cover your costs from Australia and look at the risks you would face with each shipment to a country that has the death penalty for drug offences, and uses it,' said Dave, formerly of Melbourne, but then a three-year Kuta resident.

'If you were that way inclined, it would be much easier to get local supplies and get the locals to sell it for you on the streets, minimising the risk of you getting caught.'

After suffering a dramatic downturn in tourists in the wake of the Kuta bombing which killed 88 Australians in October 2002, business people were nervous about the impact that Schapelle's trial could have. A few shopkeepers told me they were afraid the verdict would affect tourist numbers from Australia.

In his paper, 'Bali: the rise and fall of a tourist industry' former University of Wollongong Professor Adrian Vickers spelt out what damage the two Bali bombings had done to the island's tourism. He said that by the late 1990s, there were more than 1.1 million tourists landing in Bali annually and that 25 per cent of these were Australians. He quoted figures that showed Australian residents' short-term monthly departures for Indonesia had fallen from 32,200 in November 1998 to 15,100 in August 2006. It is impossible to quantify the effect of Schapelle's arrest and 20-year sentence, but coming between the 2002 and 2005 bombings and with all its high profile media coverage, it certainly would not have helped fill planes flying out of Australia for Bali.

'Some Aussies tell me they will not come back if Corby gets a big sentence and they'll tell their friends not to come to Bali,' said a restaurateur. He said the case had been bad for Bali's image. 'All the world think we are Third (World) people because of how Corby has been treated,' he said.

On Thursday, May 26, 2005—the eve of Schapelle's verdict day, some of us went to check out the courtroom where her fate would be decided. Outside there were TV crews running about all over the place and heaps of heavy TV wiring snaking everywhere as Australian Channels Seven and Nine prepared for a live broadcast on May 27.

Inside the small, stuffy courtroom, my eyes kept coming back to the small metal chair in the middle of the room where Schapelle would be seated on the most important day of her life. Next to that chair was equally plain metal swivel chair where Eka, her interpreter, would utter in English the words that would shape the destiny of the young woman who had captured the hearts of so many Australians.

In front of the chairs was a long table covered in green velvet with three ornately carved, high-backed chairs where the presiding judges would deliver the verdict, watched by an estimated million-plus Australians. The defence team was to be seated on the right hand side of the court behind a smaller, green velvet-covered table. The prosecution would be opposite them. Even though the court was empty, there was an expectant feel about it, heightened by the hustle and bustle outside, and I felt butterflies in my stomach as I took it all in. Four pooled TV cameras would be set up in the court and cameras were already set up on tripods with ladders in every window. Some 150 Australian media representatives had applied to cover the hearing, expected to last about two and a half hours. Lawyer Lily Lubis told me it would be one of the biggest media events ever held in Bali.

I found out that Judge Sirait was from North Sumatra and was a Batak Christian and a former police officer who had been a judge for eight years. His fellow judges were Balinese Hindus. What chilled me to the bone was that I discovered that Sirait had presided over hundreds of cases and had never found anyone innocent.

Rosleigh and Mick Corby spent two hours with Schapelle and they said she had a 'massive hollow' in the pit of her stomach, but she was okay and would not be taking any sedatives as she wanted to be alert.

Rosleigh said for Schapelle it was worse than having butterflies in her stomach. 'She's putting on a smiley face, but I'm her mum and underneath I know she is still hurting and is scared about what she has to face,' she told me at the bungalows.

'She's scared that some type of terrorist may try and kill her with a knife on the way to court. She hasn't had a decent night's sleep since she was locked up in that dreadful place. It's not only the cramped conditions with eight others in the cell, there are frogs and thousands of crickets coming through the cell every night. Often the girls fill a bucket with the crickets which they cook and eat. And during the day, there is a steady stream of people coming to Kerobokan prison, wanting to see Schapelle, so she's just permanently tired and stressed.'

Rosleigh said Schapelle knew the verdict would be televised live in Australia and she was a bit bemused by that. 'It's not bothering her much, from where she is, she has no idea how big she's become in Australia.'

Kay Danes also visited Schapelle, though she would not say what they talked about, but she cried when she returned to the hotel, saying her first time back inside an Asian prison had opened up many bad memories.

I was on my mobile talking to the *Gold Coast Bulletin* in the early evening when Kay knocked on my door and said Mercedes was having a meeting outside her bungalow. When I arrived, Mercedes was winding up what had been a 30-minute strategy meeting with 16 family members and friends to decide how best to get through the media army and into the court the next morning. As I approached, Mercedes looked up at me and said: 'Oh, Tony, you are in car two looking after Dad.'

I just nodded my agreement and then discovered that four vehicles had been hired by Channel Nine's *Sixty Minutes*. They were taping family members at a secret location after court for the coming Sunday's program. Mercedes wound up the meeting and we went our separate ways.

It was a long and restless night and I had little sleep. I lay thinking about how Schapelle must be faring, lying in her cramped cell, probably wide awake and wondering what Friday, May 27, 2005 had in store for her. Somehow I knew deep down it was not going to be good at all.

15:
Verdict day

ON Friday, May 27, 2005 there was little if any breakfast had in the Corby camp, as food was not high on the agenda. We left the hotel in a convoy at 8.20am as per the plan from Thursday night's meeting. In vehicle two with Michael Corby, Kay Danes and myself was also Schapelle's uncle Shun Hatton. We talked about world politics and the upcoming State of Origin rugby league games between Queensland and NSW—anything but what lay ahead of us in the court in Denpasar.

We arrived at the court at 8.55am and, as planned, formed a rugby scrum around Mick Corby as we made our way through an amazing number of television, radio and print media representatives. I did not see much of that walk as I spent most of the time with my head down watching the ground to avoid tripping on anything, calling out to the others in the group to watch out for gutters and other obstacles.

The media pack was fierce, pressing in on us from all sides as we moved slowly forward, inching our way to the court room. I actually felt physically threatened, which is unusual for me as I'm a big guy.

Once inside we took the front two rows of the public gallery on the right hand side of the court and I sat directly behind

Rosleigh, who handed me a small fan and some moist towelettes, which were welcome in the stifling heat. Schapelle, her hair tied neatly and conservatively dressed, was led into court by Balinese police at 9.08am. She smiled at Rosleigh and Mercedes sitting next to her mum, then Rosleigh blew her a kiss.

TV and still cameras peered from every vantage point in the room, and at each court window—at least half a dozen lenses were trained on Schapelle, the family and the judges. I know it's a cliché, but you could have literally cut the air with a knife. I have never been anywhere else in my life where the atmosphere weighed so heavily on me. At this stage Schapelle, alone in the centre of the room, appeared quite composed.

At 9.25am, the three judges strolled into the court in their imposing red and black cloaks with white bibs. Schapelle's translator Eka joined her in the middle of the room and Judge Linton Sirait, sitting behind a sign that said 'Ketua' which means head judge, hammered his gavel three times for proceedings to start at 9.30am. It was 11.30am in Australia and the live TV broadcasts had begun. Judge Sirait spoke for about 30 minutes, going through the charges and the evidence presented to the court by the prosecution.

Australian audiences were meant to hear Eka's translation to Schapelle, but her microphone failed and only Schapelle could hear her translations for most of the hearing. After that first half hour, Schapelle grew tenser, clenching her hands together and shaking them up and down. At 10.10am, a reporter banged his ID card on a locked side door of the court room, trying to get the police officer guarding the door to let him in. Mercedes left the court briefly to tell the reporter he needed 'to find his manners.'

The second judge, Wayan Suastrawan, who took over at 10.12am, summarised the defence case and the evidence of the witnesses who appeared on behalf of Schapelle.

By now the atmosphere in the court was suffocating, the handheld fans were working overtime and empty water bottles littered the floor. Even the local police were feeling the heat and at 10.45am, they changed shifts.

As Judge Suastrawan spoke about the evidence of Victorian prisoner John Ford, two of the prosecutors began laughing. It was 10.50am, and the tension was so great, I felt like someone strong was throttling me with both hands. I was not moving a muscle, sitting perfectly still, drenched in perspiration but totally focussed.

A solitary fan whirred ineffectually in the cream coloured sweat box, and we all watched Schapelle. Her hair swept back in a black bun like a Javanese matron, she was dressed in a black blouse, ankle length pale pink slacks, pearl stud earrings. I could not even begin to imagine what was going through her mind.

The third judge, I Gusti Lanang Dauh took over at 10.55am and of the trio at the bench he was the most strident and accusing. He spoke in detail of Schapelle's flight from Brisbane to Bali via Sydney on October 8, 2004 and the discovery of the 4.1kg (9lbs) of marijuana in her unlocked boogie-board bag.

Schapelle sat through all this quite demurely, hands clasped in a triangle, forefinger to forefinger, thumb to thumb. The judges read on and on and on. Schapelle glanced around a few times at her family. The Corbys sat sad-eyed, straining and uncomprehending, with Mercedes and her husband Wayan translating to the front row of five people.

Other friends and Australian diplomats sat around me. The judge spoke of the Customs officer's claim that Schapelle refused to open her bag for them and Mercedes said 'That's lies'. It was now 11.10am and it was very clear to all of us that there was no acquittal in sight.

Mercedes' head and shoulders slumped, as did those of Schapelle, who for the first time since proceedings had begun, began looking away from the judges' bench and just staring into space. At 11.16am, Mercedes passed along a message to the Australian Ambassador to Singapore, who was present, to have a doctor ready to attend her sister, who was now shaking uncontrollably. Mercedes turned to us and said, 'This is not looking good.'

Australian tourists, again dressed for the beach and some showing their sunburn, were handing Indonesian photographers their digi-cams to send pictures home. One middle-aged woman waved an Australian flag through one of the windows. For some who came to that court, it was like being on the set of some top-rating TV reality show. But this was real life.

Then, after an hour and a half, the third judge, Judge Dauh, got into his stride and the Indonesian media got ready. The motor drives on the digital cameras were clicking crazily and Schapelle looked at the local media pack leaning through the window by the judge's right elbow and she began to cry. She began biting her lip, rocking backwards and forwards on her chair, mouthing 'No! No! She looked upwards, seemingly praying.

Then we knew why, as the judge had just uttered, 'There is convincing proof...' She knew she was gone. She wiped tears from her eyes. To her right, one of her Indonesian lawyers, Lily Lubis, knew she was gone, too. She slumped behind her desk, hands over her face.

It was getting worse. Schapelle was desperately trying to get herself under control, breathing in and out like a weightlifter going for a record attempt.

Judge Dauh had finished. Next it was again the turn of Chief Judge Linton Sirait. Schapelle was ordered to stand. She straightened her blouse, then stood to attention. It was 11.35am and Schapelle and Mercedes exchanged a long, meaningful look, steeling themselves.

Suddenly, the courtroom erupted into utter chaos. Judge Sirait announced the sentence—20 years jail, 100 million rupiah fine—and he rapped his gavel as all hell broke loose.

Incensed, their faces flushed red with anger, Mercedes and Rosleigh leapt to their feet, screaming and shouting at the three startled judges. 'My daughter's innocent and you've taken the word of a Customs officer who was lying all along. It's all bullshit,' shouted Rosleigh as I put my hand on her shoulder and tried to get her to sit down and be quiet.

Police were moving towards us and I thought if they arrested Rosleigh for contempt of court, there would be a full blown riot and people would be seriously hurt or worse, because Indonesian cops have a history of firing their guns during riots.

But Rosleigh would not be deterred. 'No I won't,' she said. 'I know what I'm saying. I'm telling the truth and everyone needs to know the truth, not this shit.'

Schapelle turned to her mother and shouted: 'Stop! Stop it, Mum.' Her face contorted by anger, she then faced the Indonesian prosecutors sitting behind a table to her left, spat words at them and spat words at the Indonesian media, who by now were trying to climb in the windows.

Four police officers were now standing over the Corby family and supporters, and we were told we would be in contempt of court if we did not calm down.

Rosleigh was having none of it. 'I'll be taking you home, Schapelle, you're innocent, I'll be taking you home.' Police officers were trying to restrain Schapelle, who was reaching out towards her family. Eventually they relented and she came across to the public section where she spoke to Rosleigh, Mick and Mercedes saying, 'I'm all right, stay calm, I'm all right.'

They all embraced with tears running down their faces.

Schapelle was led from the court, a small woman in the midst of a struggling mob of police, half-dragging, half-carrying her around the front of the court room, through heavy metal gates, past more lines of police officers as the seething, out-of-control media pack surged. Inside the court, Rosleigh was still serving it up to the judges, telling them they would never have a proper night's sleep again.

We formed a scrum to get Michael out of the court. It was harder than coming in and we really had to push hard to get through, even with the police helping us. We even had some Australian tourists screaming at the media to leave us alone.

We finally made it to the car, but not without casualties. One of our drivers suffered a fractured shoulder after being slammed into the vehicle by storming TV cameramen and a male friend of Schapelle's injured his foot, which swelled up like a balloon.

It was a very sombre journey away from the court. Two of Wayan's sisters sat in the back, crying continually, with Kay Danes trying to console them. There had been about 10 of Wayan's family in the court and they were gutted.

I rang Elaine and spoke to her briefly, but I was totally drained by all I had just witnessed. It took just 20 minutes for Schapelle to be back in Kerobokan, with its black mould and walls topped with ribbon wire and broken glass. As we sped along, I watched the local villagers working in the paddy fields and thought that Schapelle's life may end up revolving around two sure events. The rice crop—twice a year. For the next 20 years.

I had no idea where we were going, but it was further and further away from our hotel and the laptop I needed to write my story. It turned out that Channel Nine's *Sixty Minutes* had hired a secluded villa in a secure compound out of town. I did not want to be separated from the Corbys, so I decided to dictate my report by phone from the villa. It was a beautiful, open plan Balinese villa, complete with a pool, but no-one took any notice. Everyone was flat, and distraught, with waves of helplessness washing over them.

Kathryn Bonella, who was then a *Sixty Minutes* producer, was concerned when she learnt I was a journalist, but she relaxed when I assured her that I wasn't going to write anything about the *Sixty Minutes* interview.

I sat alone in another section and filed my copy to the *Gold Coast Bulletin* by phone for more than an hour, at times breaking down. At one stage one of the secretaries taking my dictation burst into tears and couldn't continue. Then we watched the family doing the pre-recorded interview and it was a very good, sensitive one because they had all calmed down a bit and had some time to gather their thoughts as they talked about the court, the verdict and the future for Schapelle.

I felt that Wayan in particular was very good, though when I finally saw what went to air, most of his response had been cut from the program.

There was still plenty of fire in Rosleigh, who had gone off earlier to an interview for *A Current Affair* with Ray Martin. In it she told Ray how much she loved Schapelle and what followed was vintage Rosleigh. Ray Martin asked her what Prime Minister Howard had to do with it and she said: 'I tell you what, that Howard better get off his arse now otherwise (US president George W Bush) will tell him to get off his arse'.

Ray Martin said: 'At one point, Schapelle was saying "Calm down, Mum."'

'Yeah, but I wanted to have my piece.' said Rosleigh. 'I'm sick of being bloody quiet. My daughter is coming home. Today is over, but it's not the bloody finish. I'm cranky now,' said Rosleigh.

Martin said: 'She was praying.'

Rosleigh answered, 'Yes, because she's innocent... and she's not going to let these Australian people, New Zealand people, the American people (who support her), she won't let them down. She's coming home to thank them.'

'What did you think would happen?' asked Martin.

'I thought she'd be coming home. I really did. In the Indonesian way, no-one is ever innocent, but I thought they would say "You've done your time, you can go home now." We had no proof to prove her innocence. From as soon as she got off that plane, that was it. I'm positive of that. Because he (Customs officer) is a liar and they don't want to prove one of their fellow men is a liar,' said Rosleigh.

To the question, 'What will Schapelle do?' Rosleigh said: 'She is standing up for her rights this time. Before she was like "yes, we will do this the Indonesian way." They didn't follow their own protocol. Everyone has law, but they will just never have a night's sleep ever again and, by God, I hope they live a long, long life.'

Asked how she felt, Rosleigh said: 'There's no word. I just wanted to jump that bloody railing, pick her up and run out with her and if they caught me, well... but I couldn't have jumped that railing anyway. I just knew I was going to explode anyway and I thought I'm sick of being quiet—quiet just to save face.'

This interview captured exactly how Rosleigh felt at that time. She was convinced that Schapelle would be coming home that day and to see it go all pear shaped was soul destroying for her.

Verdict day also marked the beginning of the decline in Schapelle's popularity. Until that time a staggering 88-90 per cent of Australians polled in numerous surveys around the country believed she was innocent. But once she was found guilty, some gullible types who had no real idea about the major differences in the Indonesian justice system, decided she must

Above: Happier times: Schapelle with brother Michael Junior and loyal sister Mercedes.

Right: A Balinese wedding: Schapelle and former husband Kimi, with her stepbrother and stepsister Meleane and James, in traditional Balinese outfits for Mercedes' marriage to Wayan in March 1999.

Below: Schapelle and her mother Rosleigh in June, 2000 in Bali, where they met up after Schapelle split up with her husband Kimi in Japan. Both women refer to the two weeks they spent together on that trip as very special.

Top right: Rosleigh's shop on the Gold Coast, where Schapelle worked to save for her trip.

The Rox

Seafood & Takeaway

Phone Orders: **5527 0554**

Sun, Mon, Tue - 10.30am to 6.30pm Wed, Thurs, Sat - 10.30am to 7.30pm Frid - 10.30am to 8.30pm
(closed)

153 Scarborough Street (opposite Fig Tree Lane)

Right: A tearful Schapelle is comforted in the holding cell at the Denpasar court on April 21, 2005 after hearing the numbing news that the prosecutors were asking for a life sentence.

Centre: A thank you note from Schapelle to Tony and Elaine for their help and their 2005 birthday gift of a sterling silver cross and chain.

Below: Journalist Tony Wilson picked up the story of Schapelle Corby with the rest of the Australian media. He wrote his first article about his fellow Gold Coaster for the *Gold Coast Bulletin* on October 11, 2004.

Above: The grimy outside walls of Kerobokan prison, home to Schapelle Corby since 2004.

Below: Schapelle's first court appearance in a Denpasar court on January 27, 2005, Indonesia. She and that defendant's chair were to become a familiar sight to Australians. She didn't know then that she would be locked up for a very long time.

Above: Schapelle is escorted into court on April 28, 2005 to make her final plea to the judges to set her free. She hated running the media gauntlet into court. *Right*: A section of Schapelle's handwritten note outlining her final words to the judges in her defence on April 29, 2005.

firstly. I would like to say to the prosecutors, That I can not admit to a crime I did not commit.

And to the judges — My life at the moment is in your hands, but I would prefer it was in your hearts.

- I say again, that I have no knowledge of how the marijuana came to be in my bag.

I beleive the evidence shows...

1. There is a problem in Australia, with security at airports, and baggage handling procedures.

2. My only mistake is not putting a lock on my luggage.

3. I have never at any stage claimed ownership of the plastic bag and it's contents.

4. Had the police weighed all my luggage for the total weight, It would have proven to show a difference from that of the total weight at check in at Brisbane Airport.

Above: The first verdict: Michael Corby senior is corralled by the media outside Kerobokan prison on May 26, 2005, the day before her verdict. The difference in his hearing and physique in one year became marked as his health seriously declined.

Left: Tony Wilson visits Schapelle in the yard at Kerobokan in July 2005.

Above: Evidence destroyed! Police and prosecutors burn the marijuana, boogie board, fins and boogie board cover that were central to Schapelle's case on March 17, 2006. They were never tested.

Left: A thoughtful Schapelle in court for her final appeal hearing on August 25, 2006.

Notes from a prisoner: A note sent to Tony Wilson and his wife Elaine by Schapelle during a jail visit in March, 2006. She was bedridden with a severe case of conjunctivitis, known locally as 'red eye'.

Below: Schapelle uses a new public phone installed in the visiting area of Kerobokan in February 2008. As usual the centre of media attention.

A gaunt Schapelle sits in a room in Sanglah Hospital on June 25, 2008 where she was treated for depression for almost three weeks.

be guilty because she was found so by a court, no matter what the circumstances.

This simplistic view was put to me when I returned to Australia. If you were to draw a graph, her support dipped that day and has gone down ever since.

The immediate Corby family was off limits to me and other media that Friday, because they had signed an agreement with *Sixty Minutes*. I did interview Schapelle's uncle, Shun Hatton, who said the family was shocked by the 'totally unjust' sentence.

'We've had a few hours to take stock of what has happened and the response is simple—the appeal process is already in action,' he told me at the villa. 'Schapelle is innocent and we are certain she will not serve 20 years in any jail, in Bali or Australia. I know it's a cliché, and yes, of course we've lost this battle, but we will win the war and Schapelle will come home to the Gold Coast and not serve a 20-year sentence.'

We all stood around the villa talking about the appeal to the High Court in Bali, which could take a few months to be decided. 'Schapelle is strong,' said Shun. 'She understands the process, she steeled herself for it and although it was terrible to hear the words 20-year sentence she knows this a long way from being the end of the road. We are confident there are flaws in the actions of the Customs officers and police that will help Schapelle's cause at the next level,' he said.

While this discussion was taking place, the woman at the centre of the maelstrom was alone with her thoughts in Kerobokan. She had asked to be left alone for a few days, but after the attempted breakout of an American male prisoner late in 2004, no visitors were allowed on weekends anyway, so Schapelle was given extra food on Friday to tide her over.

But there was a huge media pack camped outside the prison, waiting for the family to appear.

Prime Minister Howard had reacted to the sentence back in Australia, saying he felt for this young woman. 'If she is guilty, I feel for her, that is a tragic mistake and a tragic act that has done so much damage to her young life,' he said. 'If she is innocent, my feelings for her are redoubled. As a father of young adult children, I know that many other mothers and fathers around Australia will, of course, feel the vulnerability that was felt by this family of this girl. The fact that we are a nation whose young travel so much—it is an issue that has touched this country very directly.'

Whatever platitudes were uttered by the Australian PM, they cut no ice with Rasiah. He said it was essential that the Australian Government and the AFP helped the defence team come up with evidence to support her defence that the drugs were planted in her bag. Then he went into familiar territory, saying the Australian Government should have done a lot more to assist the case during the trial and that claims by the government it had done as much as it could smacked of them 'covering their arses'. 'What is happening now in Canberra is unfathomable,' he said.

Indonesia's Attorney-General, Abdul Rahman Saleh and the Balinese prosecutors, all announced to the media in Jakarta that they felt the sentence was too lenient and that they would be launching their own appeal, seeking a life sentence.

Sixty Minutes had rented the villa for the weekend, so some members of the Corby family and friends stayed there, including a totally exhausted Mercedes. I went over there a few times and was part of a lengthy and robust discussion about whether the family should hire Harry M Miller or someone similar to look after Schapelle's affairs. I had put Harry M in touch with Shun Hatton and the legendary entrepreneur was keen to take over the matter. I felt strongly that this would be very much in

Schapelle's interests as Harry M was extremely well connected and had a very professional team which specialised in crisis management—and if this case didn't fit the bill, I don't know what did. But Rosleigh and Mercedes, in particular, were not in favour of the plan so it went nowhere.

On Sunday, May 29, 2005 I sat down with a very disconsolate but determined Rosleigh for an interview for Monday's *Gold Coast Bulletin*. She told me she didn't want Australians to boycott Bali, as had been publicly touted.

'The Balinese people are not responsible for this,' she said. 'They have had enough hurt and I don't want to see them suffer any more. We've had a great deal of support from Wayan's family and the Balinese community in general. I am asking Australians instead to boycott Qantas, and I mean the domestic and international flights, all of them, and use other carriers as it is partly through them that my daughter is in the position she's in. I would also like the Australian people to vent their anger at Jakarta, because that is where the decisions were made that led to this terrible sentence. This did not happen in Bali.'

At the time I was not sure if Rosleigh was right about the Jakarta angle, but time proved her to be correct.

Rosleigh then told me I was coming with them to the jail next day to meet Schapelle.

16:
Schapelle in Kerobokan three days after the verdict

THE Sunday papers across Australia had been full of Schapelle's case and her circumstances in prison. Sydney *Daily Telegraph* reporter Cindy Wockner had interviewed Head Judge Linton Sirait who told her he had slept well, a response to comments made by Rosleigh in court after the verdict. He described the trial as a 'crying competition' and said it was the first case he had been involved in where defence lawyers cried openly in court. 'I am responsible to God for my verdict, not people,' he said.

There was talk in the media about people boycotting Bali and Indonesia's national carrier Garuda cancelled a few flights. The Indonesian embassy and consulates in Australia were flooded with angry calls and people were even refusing to donate to the Salvation Army's Red Shield Appeal without assurances the money would not go to Indonesia. Australian travellers were wrapping their baggage in plastic, using padlocks and going to some trouble to make certain they were secure. Supporters were also planning a national day of protest on July 10, Schapelle's birthday.

In Schapelle's book *My Story,* it was reported that Rasiah had asked Mercedes to come to a meeting in his office on the night of May 28, 2005, where he told her that he had visited Schapelle in Kerobokan that day to ask her to sign paperwork saying she was happy with her lawyer's performance and would like them to continue to represent her.

Schapelle had asked for space to be alone from time to time since her arrest so she could work out whatever her demons were at a given time in the prison, and then re-group. At other times she needed extra support, but overall it highlighted her strength to combat her situation. Although time has eroded that strength to some degree, Schapelle remains a fairly strong person even after four years in jail.

The Sunday papers depicted Kerobokan prison as a hell hole with pictures. They claimed inmates were racially abusing Schapelle, that life expectancy in the jail was 10 years because AIDS was rife and drug use rampant and unchecked among its then 525 inmates, of whom 62 were women. I found out for myself that most of what they said was fairly accurate.

Apart from an early TV interview while Schapelle was still in the cells at Polda police headquarters, a few snatched words here and there from holding cells at court, and an interview with a Sydney radio journalist, I was the first print journalist to interview her and certainly the first media person to speak to her after the conviction. While conscious of all that, my main concern was to find out how she was faring after the ultimate nightmare of the verdict day.

The day started with the usual ritual of that time, with Rosleigh going to an Indonesian restaurant where her metal container would be filled with freshly made spring rolls and boiled rice for Schapelle's breakfast. Then Rosleigh and Mick, together with Rosleigh's partner Greg Martin and I, went to a supermarket to stock up on fresh food—including Schapelle's favourite mandarins and watermelons—and cigarettes to take to Kerobokan. We arrived at Kerobokan shortly after 10am and the waiting media quickly surrounded us.

Rosleigh and Greg, carrying the shopping bags and hot food, quickly got through the heavy wooden door, but it closed before I could usher Mick inside. Fortunately, at Rosleigh's insistence, we were allowed in while the guards pushed waiting photographers and cameramen back through the door.

Our names and details were entered into the book in the entrance foyer, and then Rosleigh handed over 5000 rupiah (at the time about 80 cents) and her Queensland driver's licence. We went through a large barred door and into a room where we were searched, as were the shopping bags. Then we were escorted along a passageway where we stopped at another desk and Rosleigh paid another 5000 rupiah to another guard while an inmate sold us bottles of water. I was assured I would need the water, even for a fairly short visit. We then sat in an octagon-shaped building, watching a line of male and female prisoners, handcuffed in pairs, as their names were checked off a list before they were taken to court. Most had the vacant 'no-one's home' look unique to the incarcerated.

Once they were removed we were taken into a wedge-shaped room with fading, mouldy white paint on the walls. A trustee prisoner who had been escorting us laid a rattan mat on the floor and the food and water we had bought was laid on it. We then sat on the floor and waited for Schapelle. We had been told when we arrived that she was in the clinic.

A few moments after we sat down, a smiling Schapelle arrived, hugged Mick, Rosleigh and Greg and shook my hand. 'Thank you for everything you have done, and I again want to thank the *Gold Coast Bulletin* and the people of the Gold Coast, including my friends, for all their support,' she said.

I told her the whole nation was supporting her and she smiled as I explained the reaction across Australia since the previous Friday's verdict. 'That's just great,' she said. 'It's really people power and maybe it can really help me. I hope so.' When told of the pages of SMS, email and readers' letters in the *Gold Coast Bulletin*, she looked pleased and shook her head in amazement.

Schapelle was clear-eyed, articulate and as far removed from a cowering, suicidal person as you could imagine. She explained she had been to the clinic to get a single sleeping tablet. 'I don't like them, but I got one as an emergency in case things get too much for me at night,' she said. 'It's not fair on the eight girls in my cell if I keep them awake, so that's why I got it.'

As we sat in the corner talking, a heavily tattooed Brazilian prisoner, Rogerio Tecancha Paez, together with another man, walked over and shook our hands. Schapelle said the 48-year-old was serving an 11-year sentence for narcotics. Paez and his companion then sat down as though joining our group and although the pair were speaking Portuguese, Schapelle and her mother were fearful that the second man may have been a journalist trying to overhear Schapelle's conversation. We left the room and continued our meeting in an alcove off the corridor.

Glancing around anxiously, Schapelle explained how there were always people coming into the visitors' area trying to take her photo or talk to her, and it was making her nervous. She pointed through the window at where her cell was located, across a yard past brown lawns and empty birdcages.

'I've even had the Governor of Bali visit me there when he came to the prison one day,' she said. Then she turned to me with a mischievous look on her face and said: 'Well, do I look like what you expected?'

'No,' I replied. 'You look exactly like someone I have only ever seen on TV and you are smaller than I expected.'

'I'm not that small,' she responded. 'Look at Merc... she is really tiny.'

I told her that one of her close friends on the Gold Coast, Rob Park—known as 'The Captain'—and his crew had sent their regards. Her face lit up at the news and I said: 'The Captain said to tell you the gang thinks of you every time they have beer.'

'That would be every day then,' she said with some laughter.

Someone mentioned her birthday coming up and she said she would stay 27 until she was released.

'I certainly won't be celebrating that. I'll be staying 27 until I get out of here,' she said. 'Why would I want to celebrate anything in a place like this?' About 35 minutes had elapsed and I could tell she wanted to speak to her family privately, so I said goodbye and told her to stay strong. She came over, hugged me and said: 'Thanks again for your help. I'll stay strong and I'll win this.' I returned to the front gate unescorted, handed in my pass and was joined by her family a few minutes later.

I had asked a trustee prisoner at the door to get us a taxi for 'Corby Mum' as Rosleigh became known around the prison. He wanted money but I told him to come up with a taxi with the doors open outside the front door.

We jumped into the taxi and shut all the doors. I noticed the glazed look on the driver's face and realised he was in shock as the media had encircled his cab. 'Just go, they'll move, they are used to it,' I said with the conviction of one who knows. He kangaroo-hopped the taxi out of the prison grounds and, when clear, put his foot down while sighing and sucking in great gulps of air.

17.
Sentencing in Bali

SCHAPELLE'S 20-year sentence was then the harshest handed down to a foreigner in Bali in recent times. Mexican woman Clara Elene Umana Guatrin had received a 15-year sentence in December, 2001, for smuggling 15.22kg (33.5lb) of marijuana into the country. The 32-year-old became something of a friend of Schapelle's in the prison. Another foreigner, Italian Angione Juri, was sentenced to 15-years jail for attempting to smuggle 5.3kg (11.5lb) of cocaine—a much more serious drug.

In a comment piece in the *Jakarta Post*, chief editor Endy M Bayuni said outrage expressed by the Australian public and media had not helped Schapelle. He said she had never really faced the death penalty.

'All the death penalty cases involved a large amount of cocaine, heroin or ecstasy,' he wrote. 'The diatribes by the Australian public and media against the Indonesian legal system while the trial was in progress have certainly been unhelpful.' He said judging by Guatrin's case and the amount of drugs she had been carrying, Schapelle should have been given three or four years. He further said the Denpasar District Court inadvertently tried her case as a special case, which is what led to the 20-year sentence. His comments were supported by top Perth QC Tom Percy who said he had no doubt Schapelle was innocent and blamed the 'media circus' for putting pressure on her case. He said other people tried in Indonesia had received better results because 'the whole matter was kept a lot quieter'. He and fellow QC Mark Trowell had been approached by the Australian Government to assist Schapelle's legal team in preparing its appeal.

I also spoke to Rasiah on May 30, 2005 and he told me the legal team was very confident that Schapelle would be freed at the second appeal level in the Supreme Court in Jakarta. He said they planned to engage the services of 'the best Jakarta lawyer we can get' to help with the complicated Indonesian appeal process. I asked him whether it was the usual practice that a 20-year sentence could only be reduced through the appeals hearings and not allow a person to be freed.

'Normally I would say that,' he replied. 'But this is anything but a normal case. Three days after the verdict, we still don't have the written version of the verdict, which is unusual. And yet the prosecutors and other legal people involved in the case debated the issue on Bali TV four days after the verdict. We would be looking for a reasonable reduction in sentence at the first appeal level in the High Court of Bali and then to see her walk free in the Supreme Court in Jakarta.'

Rasiah said he hoped the fact the appeal process would be handled by lawyers and judges behind closed doors would 'calm down the Australian media'.

'It's another crazy aspect of this case that I've got cameras camped outside my office and we can hardly get any work done,' he said. 'If I speak to them, it's a problem and things get twisted, and if I don't speak to them it's a problem as well. And they want to know absolutely everything, to the point where I won't even raise an eyebrow if someone asks me what colour my underpants are.'

Mick Corby, Mercedes and Wayan had gone off to a remote location in Bali where there was no mobile phone reception and a very teary Schapelle received a consular visit the day after I met her. Kay Danes went back to Kerbokan and visited a number of other Western prisoners, taking them soap, water and toothpaste.

'They told me how they all felt for her and thought her sentence was pretty steep,' she said. 'They said it could have been worse because she had been caught at the airport, allegedly bringing drugs into the country, which usually gained a stiffer penalty than if you were caught with drugs on departure.'

Kay said Phongthong prison in Laos, where she and her husband Kerry spent the best part of 2000 wrongfully imprisoned, was a much tougher jail than Kerobokan. 'Here they have got much greater freedom of movement within the prison, but I'm not suggesting life for Schapelle will be easy,' she said. 'Life in any Asian prison is really hard. Sadly, I think Schapelle will be here for some time and, no matter what, it will change her. If you have continual access to money, you'll get by. If you don't you'll struggle to survive, that's the equation at this jail.'

Kay said one of the prisoners she visited, Gabriele Natale, 42, an American serving a two-year sentence for drugs, had a large knife wound on his upper arm. 'It was untreated and oozing pus and was pretty awful really,' she said. In Kerobokan, if you need medical treatment, it comes at a price like everything else, and for a doctor to come and treat Schapelle for something basic, for example, it will cost her family about $500.

I flew home at the beginning of June 2005, a different bloke from the one who had gone to Bali to hear the verdict on a fellow Gold Coaster. Soon after, a so-called Corby 'supporter' sent an abusive letter and white powder to the Indonesian Embassy in Canberra.

Although the Corbys distanced themselves from this incident, it was yet another example of how Schapelle's name and her case were magnets to a whole range of crazies in Australia— people keen to attach themselves to her name for publicity and/or notoriety. Some were less crazy and just wanted to take advantage of Schapelle's name at the time.

I rang Mick Corby in Kuta and he said Schapelle had been in high spirits during a visit by Rosleigh on June 2, 2005. 'But while they were sitting there, a guard came and told Schapelle she must go to the office and take a call from her lawyer, Lily Lubis,' he said.

'Rosleigh said Schapelle came back shattered—shocked by the news of this white powder stuff in Canberra. She is still coming to grips with this terrible sentence and is starting to understand how important the appeal process will be to her future. She wants everyone in Australia to know that the bloody lunatic or lunatics that did this are no true supporters of Schapelle. She is scared now that this will be a black mark against her when the new judges sit down and review her case.

'We are all still angry and we understand why our fellow Australians are the same, but just like we've been told to chill out, I'm begging all Australians to do the same and let the lawyers get on with their job. If these people say they care about Schapelle, they shouldn't be doing anything that might hurt her. Things have got completely out of hand and we have been advised to put a media blanket on this whole thing for now, and I would urge Schapelle's friends and relatives in Australia to respect our wishes on this.'

Schapelle's legal team had asked for her security at the jail to be upgraded. 'We have called the prison officers and asked them to provide extra security and make sure Schapelle is okay and they have agreed to do so,' said Vasu Rasiah.

'She is very upset because it is not all positive, this can't help the case, or help Australians or help Indonesians. Whichever way you look at this incident, it is a negative incident, there is not one positive impact.' It is highly unlikely that prison officials did anything about upgrading security, and certainly there was nothing visible that Schapelle noticed.

Also in June, Perth QC Mark Trowell visited Schapelle to discuss the appeal with her. He told her he had arranged the free services of a top Jakarta lawyer to help them. No-one was quite prepared for the Hotman.

18:
Enter Hotman Paris Hutapea

HOTMAN... the name was very apt. Hotman Paris Hutapea, the highest flyer in legal circles in Jakarta—and probably Indonesia—joined Schapelle's legal team on June 7, 2005. He told me by phone from Jakarta that he also had a great deal of experience with criminal cases. 'It's true that I appear for 90 per cent of Indonesian conglomerates, but I have also done a number of high profile criminal cases in Jakarta over 25 years, involving some of the city's best known families,' he said.

'I am happy to appear for the girl for free as I don't need either the money or the publicity. I have enough of both—but I love the legal challenge and now I only have a week to read the case. We will have to go into the appeal in the High Court in Bali with a different strategy and, of course, we will have different judges. And you must make it clear we need more help from the Australian Government. It's crazy to believe this heavy weight of drugs got through so many airports in a boogie-board bag and I would like to see the High Court reopen the case for additional evidence. And then we would need all the Customs and Immigration officers working at Brisbane Airport on October 8 last year to come to Bali and testify. I know that is a big thing to ask, but with the co-operation of both governments, it can be done. I am waiting for papers to be couriered to me now so that I can officially join the team and start work.'

The flamboyant lawyer has a Sydney law degree at the University of Technology. 'Then I worked in a top international law firm in Jakarta for 20 years,' he said. Hutapea opened his own law firm in Jakarta in 1999 when the financial laws changed and he has made millions of US dollars since.

Speaking to me from his luxurious 18th floor office in the Summitmas Tower in central Jakarta, he told me he had followed Schapelle's trial in the Indonesian media. 'It will be hard to win, but it can be done and I am serious about the law and I can hold my own against anybody, anywhere,' he told me quietly.

I asked him if it was true he carried two handguns—a pearl-handled Walther PPK in a hip holster and a Beretta Tomcat in an ankle holster on his left ankle, and he replied: 'Yes, I'm fully licensed. I make enemies every day when I sue people and by taking the Corby case, I will make many enemies in Indonesia because people here want to see her behind bars for life, and there will be enemies in Bali too, because I'm an outsider.'

However he admitted his body was adorned with expensive bling, from a dazzling $175,000 diamond around his neck to massive opal and diamond rings, a diamond bracelet and gold and diamond watch. 'It is my thank you to myself for 25 years of hard work—it has all been my own sweat,' he said.

Hutapea flew to Bali and went to Kerobokan to meet Schapelle and file her appeal. He said he wanted the Australian Government to organise a new team of witnesses to be flown to Bali for a new hearing, including two prisoners named by Victorian prisoner John Ford only as Paul and Terry, plus former prisoner Ronnie Vigenza, who Ford had claimed owned the drugs.

The prosecutors lodged their appeal on June 13, 2005, again

calling for a life sentence to be imposed, saying Schapelle had committed a 'transnational crime', with drug importing a great danger to the community, which was deserving of a severe penalty.

Meanwhile, Rasiah and the two Perth QCs were not exactly getting on like a house on fire. Trowell had complained that he and Percy had not yet seen transcripts of the trial proceedings and that the pair had been disappointed with the belated nature of requests to the Australian Government by the Indonesian lawyers. But Rasiah claimed to me on June 15, 2005 that all requested paperwork had been supplied to the QCs. He had also supplied a wish list to the Australian Government, only to have that list denigrated by the barristers.

He went even further on the attack, claiming Trowell and Percy were 'political and Liberals' who had become involved in the case at the Australian Government's request to operate damage control because of the bad publicity the Australian Government had received from the case thus far. Rasiah even had a snipe that it was the QCs who had suggested that Hutapea come into the picture in the appeals stage of the case, yet they had attacked his strategy of bringing in TV soap star Hapsari to help swing public opinion.

Rasiah said it was a critical time in the case and everyone needed to get behind his legal team and all 'row together'. 'If my house is on fire, I can't help my neighbour's house,' he said. 'For this to work, there must be one head, not five, and it just makes me sick to see the QCs act like this. I have one objective and that is to get this girl out of jail. Frankly, I don't have time for this street fighting. We have a strong team and a strong case and I am grateful to Hotman for his role, but Bali Law Chambers is in charge of this case and I will be co-ordinating the appeal and Lily Lubis will be head counsel.'

It was soon to be revealed that the Howard Government had agreed to pay Bali Law Chambers $US96,000 (then $A126,000) for Schapelle's legal costs for her original trial. Lily Lubis admitted that they already received a cheque for $US46,160 and she complained that they had to make a further application for the balance. The monies were drawn from the Special Circumstances Overseas Scheme that came under the umbrella of the Federal Attorney-General.

There was a mixture of sadness, frustration and anger in the Perth silk Mark Trowell QC's voice as he explained to me that the only papers he had been sent by the Bali lawyers were the judges' summations in Indonesian. 'All we wanted to do is help a girl who is in prison,' he said.

The infighting was making Schapelle's family and friends very uneasy. In WA's legal circles, there was a saying that if you could not secure Percy or Trowell to defend you, then your best alternative was to plead guilty. Close mates since their uni days, the pair ate, drank and slept law and to my way of thinking, Schapelle's case was right up their alley. Trowell had looked after big names in the West, including millionaire businessman Abe Saffron and leading socialite Gina Rinehart, as well as taking on the case of Bali Nine member Scott Rush. He had also represented the Law Council of Australia as an observer in some high profile Asian trials.

Then on June 21, 2005, Rosleigh spoke to the (now defunct) *Bulletin* magazine. Rosleigh said that Ron Bakir had 'told her at that early visit that [Schapelle] was going to have give him $500,000 but told her not to worry as she would have plenty of time to pay it back when she was freed,' said Rosleigh.

Bakir told *The Bulletin* magazine that if he was not repaid any money for his role in Schapelle's defence, then 'so be it.'

'There was a discussion that took place between me and the

family,' he said. 'I said if I can recoup any money, then thanks. If I can't then so be it.'

Rosleigh said she and Mercedes did not even know until after the May verdict that the Australian Government had footed the bill for the Bali lawyers. Ron Bakir paid for Bond University Professor Paul Wilson and Brisbane baggage handler Scott Speed's fares to Bali. Professor Wilson confirmed that Bakir also paid for two nights' accommodation for him and made up for lost wages for Speed. Bakir and Tampoe rented a villa when they stayed in Bali.

Bakir told me: 'I have spent a lot more on this than I had expected, on lawyers, QCs, private investigators, you name it.' In the *Gold Coast Bulletin*, I challenged him more than once to provide me and the newspaper with an itemised account of his expenses on Schapelle's case. Senior Corby family members told Ron Bakir on the evening of June 21, 2005 that his services had never been asked for and the family no longer wanted to have any association with him.

On June 26, 2005, Channel Nine's *Sunday* program aired a lead story titled: 'Schapelle Corby: A legal circus.' In that program, Tampoe claimed: 'I know that Ron Bakir did a number of deals for the Corby family and the Corby family have made a substantial amount of money from those deals, and I know for a fact that Ron Bakir hasn't profited one cent from any of those monies. So from where I'm sitting, the only people I've seen who are profiting from Schapelle Corby being in jail is the Corby family.' Later in the interview Tampoe claimed Rosleigh and the family had earned 'in excess of $100,000' before the May 2005 verdict.

Another twist emerged in June 2005 in the Corby case. It turned out that a South Australian man was trying to recruit mercenaries to break Schapelle out of jail and move her out of Indonesia to a secret hideaway. On a mercenary website called

Global Guerrillas, the following message had been posted by someone calling themselves Mark on April, 21, 2005: 'Wanted: ex-special forces. I am currently looking for special forces or ex-special forces personnel in regards to a possible rescue mission in Indonesia. You must be able to pre-plan operation from beginning to end, provide any arms or paraphernalia needed and organise actual rescue attempt. Payment negotiable. This is obviously a one-off operation. PLEASE NOTE: This is a genuine advertisement and am ONLY looking for people from special forces ie SAS, SEAL, Delta Force, Rangers, Spetnaz etc. If you do NOT have this level of experience please do not reply. Only serious enquiries. I am a private individual and have contacted several PMC companies but all unable to help because of legal barriers. Rescuee is (innocent) female and currently on trial for supposedly smuggling marijuana. Drugs were placed in wrong bag (her bag) at Brisbane Airport (Australia) and X-ray (which should have picked up these drugs) was 'not working' this day. Federal police claim Indonesians will not let them fingerprint the bag. Indonesian counter claim this. Life sentence was requested by the prosecution today. Operation only to possibly proceed if found guilty. Please contact ASAP. More information with initial email contact.'

Although Schapelle was not mentioned by name, it was clear she was the 'rescuee'. The mystery man was reported to be a Mark Streater who told the *Melbourne Herald Sun* that he had the resources to carry out the operation and by June had secured recruits. He said the rescue attempt was '100 per cent do-able' and insisted the breakout plan was genuine. 'I have no doubt someone will get her out of the country,' he told *The Herald Sun*. An AFP spokeswoman said it was aware of the plan and was 'assessing the situation'. Streater said he believed Schapelle was innocent.

Rosleigh and Mercedes were both mortified when told of this situation, and terrified that some group would take Schapelle out of Kerobokan against her will. 'If that happened she would really be a fugitive and she could never come home,' Rosleigh said to me. 'We have to stop these people, they would be doing more harm than good.'

Mercedes said Schapelle became worried about how safe she was inside Kerobokan and she feared some group would make an attempt, which could also end in her being injured or worse. This crazy twist died down quickly and Streater was not heard of again.

It left the Corby family shaking their heads in amazement and wondering what was going to happen next. They didn't have to wait long.

19:
A surprise reopening of the case

JUNE 2005 was a tumultuous time for the Corbys. The sniping between the lawyers and their associates continued, much of it in public, and it was clear that something had to give. Mercedes was tired, stressed to the max and from a number of conversations I had with her I knew she was agonising about what to do, and she was also talking about it with Rosleigh and Schapelle. Rasiah was concerned that his days with the Corbys were numbered. During a couple of phone calls, he tried to talk up the value of Bakir and Tampoe and how much they had helped and added to his Bali law team.

In one of my last conversations with Rasiah, he talked to me about Rosleigh and Mick Corby being 'loose cannons' and how he needed me to control them. 'We need you to keep them under control and away from the media, mate,' he told me. I muttered something about seeing what I could do.

I rang Rosleigh and told her about the conversation that had just transpired. She was angry and then told me quietly that changes were afoot, with Mercedes meeting with an Italian/German academic living in Bali who had made Mercedes an offer that did not include any of the lawyers involved previously. I later spoke to Mercedes and she told me about the meetings, then she gave me the number of Dr. Walter Tonetto, whom I interviewed by phone. The story on the front page in *The Weekend Bulletin* on June 25-26, 2005, announced that Schapelle had sacked her entire Indonesian legal team, including Hotman Hutapea for a Mr Tonetto.

Tonetto told me he had an Italian father, a German mother and was an Australian citizen. His academic background was in literature, with a PhD in literature from Tokyo University and a PhD in literary studies from the University of Queensland. When I quizzed him about why he wanted to help the Corbys, Tonetto told me: 'All I wanted was to be the chief strategist to help Schapelle in this case and this has all happened so fast. I didn't know all this was going to happen.' He told me that he had links to a law firm called Facta Associates based in the city of Bandung near Jakarta, but would be making an announcement about the law firm on the following day.

Mercedes told me she had been approached about a week before by Tonetto and after a number of meetings, agreed to make a total change of Indonesian legal personnel. 'Schapelle and I have been very confused by everything that has happened recently, and while it became clear that certain things had to change, it was hard to decide whether we went with this new legal team or Mr Hutapea.' Vasu Rasiah thought the change was not in Schapelle's best interests. 'At this junction, it's very bad (for the case),' was his curt reply.

My wife, Elaine, and I searched the internet for information on Tonetto. We questioned whether he should be the case's chief strategist and compared to Hutapea, with his connections and Australian law degree, we felt Mercedes and Schapelle, struggling under absolute stress, had made the wrong move.

I rang Mercedes in Bali and we talked about our doubts and I could tell she was very stressed and tired, but that she had doubts as well. We spoke for quite a while and then, later that night, Mercedes rang back and we had an even longer conversation, going over all of it again. The final upshot was that she had decided to go back to Hutapea and Erwin Siregar and forget about Dr Tonetto.

Siregar had his own law firm in Bali and had only been seconded to Schapelle's first defence team. Siregar had done the bulk of the work during the trial without any controls over strategy and direction, which had made it extremely difficult for him. So Monday's *Gold Coast Bulletin* (June 27, 2005) had the headline 'He's Back. Hotman Returns' and it explained the change of heart, with Mercedes saying Schapelle had 'hit it off' with Hutapea when he visited her and that she had respect for Siregar.

Although Mercedes had contacted Dr Tonetto and told him of the decision, he refused to accept the news. 'I am in charge of the team,' he told me when I rang him. 'Mercedes is her sister, but I was appointed by Schapelle, so I cannot accept the news at the moment.' He eventually did accept his very brief tenure was over.

Hutapea said he would be taking charge of the case immediately. 'I felt very much for Schapelle in that prison,' he said. 'She had great dignity under the circumstances, but the crazy things that have happened around her in the past eight months, have not helped at all.'

Schapelle gave Mercedes a letter she had written to Hutapea. 'You, Mr Hutapea, are a hot man and are very much needed to work your expertise, to do the best you possibly can to help me to be a free woman,' she wrote to him. 'You must think I'm a crazy Australian, but no, I'm not, just confused and disorientated.

But I know what I want now and that's for you to help me from this horrible cage I'm trying so hard to survive in.'

Mercedes also read a statement from the family to the judges and the Indonesian government. Rosleigh said if the Australian Government had helped the Corby family in selecting Indonesian lawyers from the beginning, her daughter may well have been home by then.

At this time emotions were high, allegations were being made, the many lawyers involved were stressed, intense and fighting for space. All sorts of allegations were being made in the media, while Schapelle continued to sit in her 'cage' in Bali and her family travelled backwards and forward to Australia, trying to keep her alive. Food sustenance was crucial and health issues were and still are a constant concern to the family.

Outside the prison the number of people who held their own opinions, tried to act on them, extracting media stories, kudos or genuine supporters who wanted to help, grew.

A Sydney radio station alleged they had a letter that appeared to have Schapelle pleading for Tampoe to return to the defence team. In this letter, Schapelle told Tampoe she 'needs' him and thanks him for everything he has done. The letter was real, but the timing was all wrong. Schapelle had written the letter on May 28, 2005—the day after her verdict. On that May day, Vasiah had told Schapelle that Tampoe was tired and wanted to leave the team and return home. He told her that if she wanted Tampoe to remain, she must write a letter to him, telling him she wanted him to stay. A frightened Schapelle did not want anyone to leave her team at that stage, so she wrote the letter.

After it became national news, Schapelle asked Mercedes to fax a letter to me at the *Gold Coast Bulletin* explaining when she wrote the letter. 'I have not written another letter to Mr Robin Tampoe,' she told me in the letter. 'I do not wish Mr Tampoe to be on my defence team any longer, regards Schapelle Corby.'

In a move that caught everyone by surprise on the afternoon of July 4,2005, Bali High Court Chief Judge Made Lingga ordered that the Corby case be reopened in the district court. This naturally pleased Schapelle, her family and friends and the new legal team and it seemed that Hutapea's skills were already paying dividends.

Judge Lingga said there is 'a possibility of freedom if her alibi is true'. Her main Bali lawyer Erwin Siregar said the reopening was 'truly fantastic for us'. He said the High Court judges hearing the appeal had reopened the case under Article 240 of Indonesian law. Called *putusan sela* it meant this would not be a total retrial, but rather it would just hear new evidence.

'This basically says the appeal judges do not 100 per cent believe the result of the original case and want more done, so the defence can bring new evidence and witnesses,' Siregar said. 'But now it's extremely important that the Australian Government helps us by getting witnesses available for the reopening as soon as possible.'

Mercedes said it was 'critical that we take full advantage of this opportunity to prove once and for all that Schapelle is innocent as we have said all along'. She could not tell Schapelle until the next day and she said Schapelle sat in stunned silence at first, which was followed by a big smile.

'She was surprised, well sort of surprised because I think deep down, she thought this might happen,' she said. 'She's such a positive person. And even though I'm not happy about her facing those same three judges, Schapelle just said: "I'll be fine, I don't mind". She's not very happy about having to go back to court through the media scrum again. That was something she really hated, but she knows she has to do it.'

Mercedes said Schapelle immediately penned a letter to Prime

Minister John Howard telling him the news was 'absolutely fabulous' and asking his government to co-operate with her legal team. Hutapea said he had asked his client to write to Mr Howard. He also flagged plans to call up to a dozen Australian witnesses, including Ronnie Vigenza who had been accused of owning the drugs found in the bag. Vigenza, who continued to deny any knowledge of the business, said he was glad Schapelle had been given a retrial. 'I find it strange that there are baggage handlers and other people involved and I'm still the number one suspect,' he said.

Justice Minister Chris Ellison said the Australian government would consider granting immunity from prosecution to anyone who admitted putting the drugs in Schapelle's bag and that they were looking at the possibility of getting witnesses to appear in the case via a video link. Hutapea warned that teleconferences had few precedents in Indonesian law and that the law in that country did not recognise immunity. Mr Ellison added that the Federal Government had written to Brisbane and Sydney Airports, plus Qantas, about offering assistance at the retrial.

Brisbane Airport Corporation corporate relations manager Jim Carden told me they would co-operate, but he doubted they could produce any substantial evidence. Qantas and Sydney Airport Corporation both indicated they would co-operate with the new defence team.

In a frank interview, Hutapea told me that he planned to ask the Bali High Court whether he could re-examine the evidence of a Customs officer whose testimony was crucial in Schapelle's drug conviction. Gusti Winata's account that Schapelle said the marijuana was hers, which she denied saying, was the linchpin in the prosecution's case and Hutapea wanted to put that testimony to the sword.

'I would like to have Mr Winata's knowledge and understanding of English put to a test in court as it may well be that his English was not sufficient to understand that Ms Corby was only referring to the bag and not the marijuana as hers,' he said.

He also urged Qantas staff working on the day of Schapelle's arrest to come forward and testify. 'By saying they saw nothing unusual, these people can help me build a case that there is overwhelming reasonable doubt and this could well see Ms Corby a free woman in Bali.' he said. 'But at the moment I have nothing and we can't have the case reopened without witnesses. These Qantas staff have nothing to fear if they saw nothing, but they could be a big help to a fellow Australian facing 20 years in jail.'

Hutapea said he was trying to buy some more time for the reopening as July 20, 2005 was too soon for him to get organised and he hoped to get the date put back to the first week in August.

Prime Minister John Howard wrote a three-page letter to Schapelle, dated July 9, 2005, telling her his government would help clear her name. But he said the government 'cannot force witnesses to give evidence. I feel for you and your family at this very difficult time,' he wrote.

'The Bali High Court's decision to allow new evidence in the Denpasar District Court is a welcome opportunity for you and your legal team to present additional evidence in your defence. The Australian Government is monitoring your case closely. Let me assure you that the Australian Government will continue to provide every assistance it can under our legal system, consistent with our approach to date. Finally, I would like to assure you that I will continue to take a personal interest in your case.'

Meanwhile, I was about to go back to Bali with Rosleigh to be there for Schapelle's birthday, even though she planned to stay the same age while inside prison. I was looking forward to meeting her again.

20:
A birthday
in prison

I SAT next to Rosleigh on the flight to Bali and learnt about her life, gaining a real insight into her makeup as she opened up to me about her awful childhood and an extremely difficult mother. Family love and values had begun for her when she started her own family and it was now easy for me to understand what made her tick and why family was everything to her. She may have been formally educated only until Year Six, but there is a lot to admire and learn from this woman and her public, rough-edged persona is far removed from the real person that is Rosleigh.

Schapelle's birthday fell on a Sunday, so she could have no visitors on the actual day, but we planned a special visit on the Monday morning. Rosleigh was loaded with presents. Before going to Kerobokan, we went to Bali Deli and bought some special treats, then we headed to the jail and the inevitable waiting media pack.

In my report in the *Gold Coast Bulletin*, I called it a picnic in a prison, which didn't impress Rosleigh. She didn't say anything to me, but she told other media later that it was not a picnic. I understood what she meant about prison not being a picnic, yet in many ways it had that feel about it. Sushi, rice crackers and dips, tempting cakes from the deli, together with soft drinks and water were laid out on bamboo beach mats under the shelter of two umbrellas in a very hot prison courtyard. Schapelle sat cross-legged wearing three-quarter-length pants, a blouse and a baseball cap. 'I haven't washed my hair for a couple of days. That's why I'm wearing the cap,' she said with a giggle.

There was a change to Schapelle since I had seen her after her sentence horror. Then, on May 30, 2005, her face was fringed with lines of stress and worry as she contemplated her bleak future.

But now, five weeks later, on July 11, although officially a year older at 28 years, she looked younger and those worry lines were gone. This was a confident and more assured Schapelle among her family and friends in a low-key gathering to mark her birthday. Although Schapelle had said she would not celebrate anything inside prison, Rosleigh was determined that her daughter 'should have some nice things, even in that dreadful place'.

So while everyone ate and drank, Schapelle received a sterling silver watch, white gold earrings, some clothes from Rosleigh including a black and white suit to wear to court for her unexpected, but gratefully accepted, re-hearing in a few weeks. There were heaps of mail and birthday cards from well-wishers in Australia and other gifts including a tapestry of an old church, hand-made teddy bears and jewellery.

On that Monday, Schapelle was relaxed. 'I'm a lot more comfortable with the decisions I've finally made and very happy about my new legal team and my chances,' she said.

Generally we steered the conversation away from courts and appeals and spoke of other things, then Schapelle revealed another bizarre little twist in her story. 'They're having (Indonesian) Independence Day in the prison on the 17th (of July) and the woman in charge of the women's section has chosen me to be in the 10-person aerobics team,' she told me.

'I thought it would have been silly to say no. It's a bit of fun really, and a break from the daily routines. We've already had some practices and there's more to come, although they haven't chosen any music yet. I'm going to be dressed in Indonesian national costume and the Governor of Bali will be here to watch our presentation.'

Schapelle looked trim and said she had worked hard in the past nine months to keep herself mentally and physically fit. 'I fill two empty water bottles with stones and I use them as dumb bells to exercise at six in the morning before our cell is opened and then just after 4pm when we are locked down,' she said. 'I also cut the cigarettes back to three or four a day, which is all I used to have before all this happened and now I refuse to have a cigarette after 2pm each day, I just pray and the cravings go away.'

At that stage in 2005, the support and compassion from her fellow Australians amazed and buoyed Schapelle. She was receiving up to 300 letters and cards daily and this included poems, prayers, presents and even a number of marriage proposals.

'I never realised how many good people there were before all this happened to me,' she said. 'I had my family and my circle of friends on the Gold Coast and I guess I never really thought about whether other people were good or not, but now it amazes me every single day.' She said the letters helped sustain her in that dire prison.

'In all those thousands of letters and cards, there's only been one person that said nasty things about me and I think it might be because he'd written before and had not received a reply,' she said. Schapelle said it was difficult to reply to the mountain of mail she was receiving.

'People have to understand that it is difficult in here, when I'm locked up every day at four o'clock and I don't have electricity or a desk or anything like that.'

Schapelle still receives a steady stream of mail, although it's nothing like it was in 2005, and she replies to most of it. These days, she has to pay to get her mail, which is not surprising as everything in Kerobokan comes at a price, with the inmates even having to pay rent for their cells.

Those Monday and Tuesday visits in July 2005 were the best I had seen Schapelle at that stage—the re-trial news had really given her a great deal of hope and it showed. But there was an unpleasant subplot being played out over those same days with Mercedes' former best friend, Jodie Power.

The friendship had become rocky in 2005 for a number of reasons, mainly because Power had started a fund for Schapelle which I had publicised at her request.

The other source of friction was that she had stayed in Bali for some months, to assist Mercedes with Schapelle. At that time Jodie was experiencing difficulties in her marriage, but Mercedes felt that she had overstayed her welcome. Power had travelled to see Schapelle and give her birthday gifts from a magazine's readers, with a story to follow. She had gone to the prison on the Sunday but was refused entry. Mercedes had already told her there would be no Sunday visit. Power tried to see Schapelle on the Tuesday, however Schapelle refused to come to the visitors' area to see her.

At the same time, a rally involving about 100 Schapelle supporters took place at a park in Tugun on the southern Gold Coast. Schapelle had been able to get a friend to text the gathering with the message: 'Thanks guys. Remember every day is a new day and every day is a present'. The gathering urged the Federal Government to do more and then held a fundraising barbecue.

There were doubts about the prospects for Schapelle's retrial, with the Federal Justice and Customs Minister Chris Ellison saying they could not give immunity to witnesses because it would violate national laws. AFP Commissioner Mick Keelty had also declined a request to give evidence at the re-trial.

Our next visit to Schapelle, on July 13, found her pacing and shaking in anger. The source of her anger was a visit to the jail by local media. Schapelle explained that 14 legislators from the Indonesian House of Representatives went to Kerobokan to look at security, plus legal and human rights issues. They were accompanied by about 30 local media, including TV cameramen, photographers and reporters.

Schapelle had been praying in the chapel and knew it was nearly time for family and friends to come and visit her in the afternoon. So she walked into the sunlight, only to be confronted by the media pack.

'They all started running towards me and I felt, what do I do now? I can't roll out the red carpet for them, so I just ran into an office and hid behind a desk,' she told me, still shaking with anger.

'Obviously I know how much they want to get shots of me and I knew I was filmed quite a lot during rehearsals for Indonesian Independence Day and I thought, I suppose I can put up with this for five or 10 minutes. But I ended up crouching behind the desk for 90 minutes and still they wouldn't go away and I could just hear them saying "Corby, Corby, Corby" over and over again.

'The guards were doing nothing when they should have been protecting me and finally I couldn't handle it anymore so I decided to slip out the back door of the office and make a break for the administration area to see the prison boss and make a complaint.'

She sprinted across a concrete and grass courtyard area where prisoner visits are conducted on hot days and tried to go through a big green metal gate that led into the administration area, but it was locked.

'I climbed onto the gate and I was swearing and yelling at the guards, "Why aren't you doing something to help me" and I was swearing pretty badly because I was just so angry. The guards surrounded me and grabbed me off the gate and of course all this was being filmed and photographed and I know bad this must look.' At this point, I noticed there were red marks on her arms where the guards had grabbed hold of her as they peeled her off the metal gate.

Schapelle said the media thing was 'totally crazy'. 'They are really, really stalking me and I am sure I still have some rights in that regard,' she said. 'I am just so sick and tired of this happening all the time. I have even had guards around the place with disposable cameras. And I have enough on my mind with my appeal and my situation without having to wonder every waking minute whether someone is going to film or photograph me in what is supposed to be a secure area.'

After the media had left, Schapelle took some deep breaths, then went back to her cell to prepare for our visit, only to find out that the media had been in the cell as well. 'The girls told me they were in there for ages photographing my things, moving them around and asking the girls questions about me,' she said. 'Surely that cannot be right. Obviously I don't know about Indonesian law, but in Australia that would be a very obvious and serious breach of my privacy. I suppose some people will accuse me of overdoing it, but I ask them to imagine themselves in my position and hope that most people will be sympathetic to my situation. I am looking forward to my appeal day, but I'm not looking forward to having to run the gauntlet of this vile media pack who seem intent on making my life a total nightmare.'

Schapelle calmed down a bit as she sat and ate an Aussie-style pizza with Rosleigh, her aunt Sandra Corby and myself that she knew would be all over the Australian media in a few hours. Before we left she asked me to contact her lawyers, Hotman Hutapea and Erwin Siregar. At the time, they were holding a four-hour meeting about her case in Jakarta with up to 16 people involved, including law professors, as they fine-tuned their plans and strategy for the re-hearing in the Bali District Court in Denpasar the following week.

'Please ask them to ring the prison,' said Schapelle. 'I want them to make a very serious protest about this matter as I feel strongly that I was set up and pushed to the point where it would make me look bad. I know I've lost many rights and privileges as a prisoner in this place, but now I have become the star in a freak show and this will have me portrayed as a feral animal and I assure you and everyone reading this, that it is not true. I haven't lost it all together.'

Schapelle who, like Mercedes, had become quite media savvy, knew the *Gold Coast Bulletin* was part of the News Limited group, and she asked me if I could get this story in other papers in the group and I told her I would try. 'Go and make me look good,' she said, laughing, as I left the prison.

That night we watched the Balinese news and she looked pretty wild. They had not beeped out her language and she had used almost every swear word in the book. They also had close-ups of her belongings and these were in the newspapers the next day. The Balinese media claimed they had only wanted to give Schapelle the chance to speak about conditions in Kerobokan prison.

Siregar went to see the prison governor to discuss the incident the next day and Mercedes lodged a formal complaint with the Australian Consul-General in Bali, Brent Hall. She said if the media wanted to speak to Schapelle, then they should have approached her lawyer Erwin Siregar. 'And although the politicians have the right to inspect the cell, there was absolutely no way the media had the right to handle and photograph her personal belongings,' said Mercedes.

Schapelle was much calmer the next morning; even after we told her how bad and wild she had looked on TV and in the papers. Siregar said everything was now in place for the re-hearing.

On my last visit on that trip, I spent a lot of time with Schapelle. The guards just seemed to forget about us and while Mercedes sat and read, Schapelle and I talked about a wide range of things. She even took me on a tour of parts of the prison and showed me the tower that then housed the Bali bombers Amrozi bin Nurhasyim, Mukhlas and Imam Samudra.

'There's steps going up to the top, but it's not used and there are four cells at the bottom,' she said. Then she told me that Imam Samudra stared down on her each day as she went past to the visiting area. She pointed to his cell, which was nearest to the walkway. 'He knows I come past for my visits at 10.30am and 1.30pm most days and he is always at the window staring at me,' she said. The Bali bombers were moved to another prison late in 2005 and some of the death-sentenced Bali 9 prisoners now occupy the tower cells.

Kerobokan is generally a very dreary place with an air of despondency that pervades the place, but as Schapelle showed me the rose gardens scattered around the buildings and the neatly manicured lawns, she remarked: 'It doesn't look too bad from here.' To the right of the central tower is a clinic where a doctor and nurse hold morning sessions for a fee, but they don't have much to offer in the way of medicine. Beside the drab clinic is an equally drab building that houses the worst prisoners in the jail apart from the Bali bombers.

Farther right again is another building and this time I saw a young Indonesian male prisoner hanging on the bars. He looked downcast and forlorn. 'This is where the new male prisoners are placed when they come to the jail from the police cells,' Schapelle explained.

Further left was a poorly stocked library and a canteen. Only the male inmates are allowed to use the library. Schapelle then pointed out other areas such as the women's section and her Cell 7—which is no longer her home. She told me she had become scared of the dark.

'Sometimes there are blackouts and it scares me,' she told me.

This was a real quality visit and she talked about what she missed most—a shower, a bed and to be able to walk on the beach and watch a sunset. She also talked of her hopes for a family of her own and 'a nice little house' and a nice car. Nothing too elaborate.

Then she really floored me by saying: 'Tony, when will my innocence count for something... anything?'

21.
A day in the life of a Kerobokan prisoner

DESPITE the obvious loss of freedom, the next most painful thing for inmates of most Asian prisons is the amount of time on their hands and time weighs heavily on Schapelle in Kerobokan. If she was interred in an Australian prison, there would jobs to do, courses to attend and TV to watch. Kerobokan offers virtually none of the above for Schapelle and her fellow prisoners, apart from work making handicrafts.

There was some talk in 2006 about Schapelle continuing her TAFE beautician's course which had been put on hold when she became her father's full-time carer, but as Mercedes logically pointed out, that course and all others rely heavily on computers and the internet and these things are not on the agenda at Kerobokan. Even if, by some miracle, they became available, they would only be for the use of male inmates.

Generally, Schapelle's day begins early. In the first few years in Kerobokan she always woke first between 5.30am and 6am and this was partly due to the fact that inmates in her then crowded Cell 7 were repeatedly stealing food, drinks and other items from her. This infuriated her because she was very generous with the many gifts she was receiving and handed out loads of stuff to the others. Even now, in 2008, the thieving problem still exists but it is on a lesser scale, with only four others sharing her cell, so her early rising is somewhat later. Guards open the cell doors between 7am and 7.30am and one of the first duties of the day is filling your bucket.

Ever since she first arrived in Kerobokan, there have been problems with the water pump in the women's section and even though it has been replaced, it is never repaired properly. This may not seem to be a big deal to readers, but having running water is a real luxury in showerless Kerobokan.

Once the water is sorted, Schapelle will have her morning ablutions then breakfast of cereal and milk and fruit juice. She does not drink coffee. As well as the gas powered little stove, she also has a small portable Esky (fridge) and milk, drinks, fruit and vegetables keep well in there for a few days. Mercedes and the family have always used one of the island's upmarket delis to get Schapelle's food and groceries and these days Mercedes favours Papaya—one reason being that they put ice in with the fruit and vegies for free and this helps keep them longer in the Esky.

Schapelle cooks a lot of pasta, noodles with vegies, chicken or pork. She does not eat red meat in Kerobokan at all. She still cooks for her cellmates sometimes if they want and she still tries to teach them about cleanliness, but it has always been pretty much a losing battle.

After breakfast she will wash and tidy up her section of the cell, which really means the entire cell as no-one else will help her, then maybe she will read or listen to music and read or write letters. She enjoys Wilbur Smith books for example and she has an MP3 player and a CD player to listen to music. Her music tastes are very widespread and she even likes country music, which family members tease her about.

The visiting regimen has changed from the first few years of her imprisonment when weekends were non-visiting periods, but you could go Monday to Friday. Now Sunday and Mondays are the non-visiting days, but you can visit Saturday mornings. The visiting times are from 10.30 am to noon and 1.30pm to 3pm and these days the times are strictly adhered to.

The prison tightened up after Governor Ilham Djaya took over the reins from Bromo Setyono, and while he moved on in April 2008, so far his regime rules remain. Whereas most prisoners had the run of the jail during the day in the first few years that Schapelle was an inmate, now they can stay only in their section and the visitors' area. This used to be a courtyard with a mural wall, a (dry) fountain and some rooms running off the courtyard. Early in 2007, this changed and the courtyard area was tiled and covered and it is certainly is a cleaner environment, but Schapelle says that doesn't apply to the rest of the prison. The roofed courtyard now holds all prisoners and visitors and is very crowded daily as well as being extremely hot and humid. Schapelle has a theory this is a deliberate move so visitors stay for shorter periods.

After the morning visit, Schapelle has lunch, then exercises or weaves mats or reads again. She also does embroidery and collects these items from a group of female prisoners that she is sort of in charge of as a Tamping, which is akin to being a rank above an ordinary prisoner. Then comes the afternoon visit and, if they feel like it, prisoners can come and visit with another prisoner's visitors if they don't have any visitors themselves. The female inmates are locked down for the night sometime between 4pm and 4.30pm. This long period of daily isolation is definitely the toughest part of life in Kerobokan.

In her new cell, for which she pays rent of around $100 per month, Schapelle has a power point and a lamp, but the power is so weak and there are so many blackouts that she doesn't read after dark, because she is afraid of damaging her eyesight in the dim light. And of course, the prisoners have to pay for the electricity. So there is much time for thinking during the lock-up period and I'm sure there are there are still many nights where the 'Why me's' and the 'What ifs' invade and destroy Schapelle's sleep.

Kerobokan is a rigid prison—it is quite clear when you are there that you are in a heavy security jail. Like any prison, there is a prisoner hierarchy—that means fights to protect your standing or whatever are quite common. Because these prisons are not as regulated as Australian ones, fights are more common than in Australia. I have seen male prisoners with knife wounds and Schapelle has been involved in a few fights with other female prisoners where she has been able to hold her ground. This may all seem awful, but people must not lose sight of the fact that this is a prison and an Asian one, where life is very cheap and it is a dog-eat-dog mentality that rules in what is a very harsh world.

Back in 2005, there was some media fallout after Schapelle's outburst over the sustained Balinese media stalking and one Australian media report, which followed Balinese reports, claimed that Kerobokan prison authorities considered Schapelle an escape risk. A bemused Schapelle told me at my next visit on July 18, 2005 that she had no intention of scaling the prison walls, topped with ribbon wire that would cut a prisoner to shreds.

'If you believe all the media reports about me, I've been frequently suicidal, pregnant and now I'm about to become an escapee,' she said. 'It's just so stupid. Why would I consider such a thing when my legal team believes I can gain my freedom on appeal? It's obviously another case of the media having nothing real to write about, so they've just asked some loaded questions and turned the whole thing into yet another work of fiction involving me.'

Schapelle said her lawyers had spoken to Governor Bromo Setyono about the previous week's media stalking incident. 'At no stage was there any suggestion that they considered me to be at risk of escaping or trying to escape,' she said. 'I mean you have to think it through logically. If I got out, and I don't know how I would do that, where would I go? I have no passport and sadly, for all the wrong reasons, I would be one of the most recognised people around Bali... the whole thing is total rubbish.'

Schapelle also scoffed at media comments that she had avoided the Balinese parliamentary delegation during the stalking issue. 'I did not know they were in the prison,' she said. 'All I saw initially was this large media pack running at me and stalking me. After I hid and tried to get away from the media, two of these people from the committee came into the room where the guards had taken me and they just stood there and stared at me. They never said a single word and after a while I yelled at them saying "what are you staring at". At no stage did I have any idea who they were or what they were doing there.'

22.
Work on the appeal continues

WORK on the appeal was gathering pace. Around this time I came across a 35-page report written by a New South Wales police officer, Detective Inspector Jason Breton, which was critical of the security at Sydney Airport. I sent a copy to Mercedes and suggested he would make a good appeal witness but she was unable to gain his services.

The legal team was also talking to a Qantas security officer from Brisbane Airport who had written to the family offering his assistance. 'It would be very useful if the Federal Government could offer an official to tell the court the truth about our airports. It's not as though they can pretend it doesn't exist when it is all over the media,' said Mercedes. 'The lawyers have told us that it carries more weight in the Indonesian legal system if it comes from a government employee with some seniority. They are also going to see if the court will allow me to testify about how I asked for the two bags—containing the 4.1kg (9lb) marijuana that someone planted in Schapelle's bag—to be fingerprinted, which never happened, and how Customs officers allowed me to take all the other bags home without even a glance at them or their contents.'

Although Hutapea knew the odds were stacked against him, he was hoping for a sentence reduction.

'The judges will want something substantial, not just talk,' he said. 'But for this to happen, the judge will have to be able to fully grasp the concept of reasonable doubt.' He said he would be pushing the appeal judges to reduce her sentence from 20 years for possession and trafficking under section 82 of Indonesia's anti-drug law to section 78, which would find her guilty only of possession. 'Having possession only has a maximum sentence of 10 years and normally people charged under this section get around six years,' he said.

On the eve of the retrial, a mystery caller made an international call to Erwin Siregar's law office in Bali. The male caller told Siregar that there was 'someone' who knew who put the 4.1kg (9lb) of marijuana in Schapelle's boogie-board bag. Siregar said the man, whom he thought had called from Australia, said the person with the information would not come forward unless granted immunity from prosecution.

Mercedes said the family was becoming frustrated because of the difficulties of getting witnesses to testify. She had been speaking to a Qantas security guard in Brisbane who had written a letter to the Corby family saying security was so lax in Brisbane that you could get a gun through the airport, but the phone line dropped out and Mercedes had not been able to get the woman on the phone ever again.

Then there was Melbourne couple Steve and Dee who went to Bali in 1997 and found compressed marijuana in their suitcase when they arrived and were told by the Australian Consulate to throw it out. They had gone public with their tale but efforts to get them to Bali to testify ultimately failed because the couple were afraid that telling their story in a Balinese court might lead to charges.

Mercedes said the legal team had tried to get Bali drug squad chief Colonel Bambang Sugiarto to testify after he told a Balinese TV program that his investigators could not complete their investigations because the evidence was tainted. 'But his superiors are unlikely to allow him to appear,' she said.

Others on the wish list to testify at the hearing were Brisbane Airport employees Goronco Trajkoski, Jela Stevanovic, Nabil Bechara, Mohamed Abbas and William Samaha, AFP officer Leticia Davidson and retired police officer Les Kennedy.

That left Jakarta law professor Indriyano Seno Adji as the sole witness at the appeal hearing, so on July 20, 2005 Hutapea asked for and was granted an adjournment until August 3, so the legal team could try to get more witnesses to testify.

At the end of July, Hutapea told me that a Victorian prisoner known only as Paul was prepared to give evidence to back another prisoner's claim that the drugs found in Schapelle's boogie-board bag were not hers. But he would only give evidence via video link if he could wear a mask to hide his identity. Hutapea said the Bali District Court could not give approval for this as they did not have the authority. 'So we will have to ask the High Court and I'm hopeful it will be allowed,' he said.

Prisoner Paul made a statement to AFP officers in which he recalled a conversation he overheard earlier in 2005 between two other prisoners, one of whom he identified as Ronnie Vigenza. Vigenza was first named by another Victorian prisoner, John Ford, as the man who owned the 4.1kg (9lb) of marijuana found in Schapelle's bag.

In Paul's statement, Vigenza said: 'Fuck Schapelle Corby, she fucking cost me four kilos of smoke'. Hutapea said that whereas Ford's testimony was hearsay, this statement was stronger, although he admitted that he did not know how much weight the High Court judges would place on it.

At the same time, a Victorian man had claimed he was the man who should have removed the marijuana stash at Sydney airport. Identified in Sydney's *Daily Telegraph*, he was reported to say: 'I was supposed to make a quid out of picking up the package but it never went ahead. I got a call telling me to forget it because the package had ended up with the Corby girl who was all over the TV. I know for a fact the drugs in Corby's bag were the drugs I was supposed to collect.'

This man was now doing the rounds of media outlets and current affairs programs trying to sell his story. A disgruntled Mercedes said that her sister's case had attracted a huge range of people hell bent on nothing else but making money from it. She said it was very clear that the man was not a credible witness. 'When he told the media he would be paid $50,000 to collect the drugs, we knew he was not telling the truth because that figure is more than what we've been told the drugs were worth on the street in Australia ($32,000),' she said.

'It's very disappointing that these people come forward claiming they have information to help us. And it's not about the truth for my sister, it's because they somehow think they can make money out of all this and I can't believe how much of it is going on.' She said there was another man in Queensland who had claimed he put the drugs in Schapelle's bag.

'We have been talking to him as well, but I don't think it is going anywhere either,' she said. 'It's crazy to have people confessing to things they did not do.'

Around this time, Rosleigh sold her takeaway business on the Gold Coast as the bills mounted in her daughter's case. 'We have to live and pay bills and I have had extra expenses getting the family to Bali and keeping them there, plus there are Schapelle's needs as well,' she said. 'I didn't have it for sale but these people came in and made me an offer, and under the circumstances, I thought it was a good idea as we need the money and I want to spend more time helping Schapelle.'

Rosleigh had owned the Southport business for about two years and had built it up into a popular takeaway with the older locals in the area. 'I'm sad I'll be leaving them, but I have more important things to worry about at the moment,' she told me. I mention the sale here mainly to make the point that this family from Struggle Street was obviously not rolling in cash.

As August, 2005 dawned, Justice Minister Chris Ellison told AAP he was becoming increasingly frustrated with Schapelle's legal team over their calls to facilitate the testimony of Australian witnesses and he added that time was running out.

Hutapea told me he had completely 'lost faith with Australia's willingness to help in the case'. Senator Ellison said the government had been pressing Hutapea on both mutual assistance and in relation to evidence by video link from Australia. 'We still haven't had an answer on the question of evidence by video link,' he told ABC radio. He said it wasn't clear what mutual assistance Hutapea had sought with the Indonesian authorities.

This was the confused backdrop to Schapelle's return to court on August 3. And when Schapelle's legal team met with Qantas staff from Brisbane on the eve of the hearing, Mercedes said she was extremely shocked.

'I was a bit sharp with them for not helping us earlier and that's when they told us that Tampoe had gone to Brisbane and spoken to the check-in staff in March, 2005 during the original trial,' she said. 'Even if the staff could only say that nothing out of the ordinary happened that October day at Brisbane Airport, it would have helped us, as the boogie-board just looked like a normal, flat board and bag at that stage, that would not have drawn second looks from anyone.'

Back in court on August 3, another shock awaited them. A quietly spoken man approached Schapelle and asked 'did she not want his services again?' Puzzled, she asked who he was and he explained he was the court-appointed interpreter and that he had sat through the original court proceedings feeling unwanted. It transpired that Eka, who was photographed so constantly in courtroom shots with Schapelle from late January to May 27, 2005, worked for Rasiah and was not an official interpreter.

Schapelle told me that Eka did not always explain things fully during those four months of hearings, sometimes telling Schapelle she would come back to something that had been said, but then failing to do so. Schapelle said during the August 3 hearing she understood the entire proceedings, which had not been the case before.

23.

The appeal struggles

NORMALLY before a court appearance, Schapelle was a bundle of nerves, but Rosleigh said that for this hearing she was in fine spirits. That buoyant mood quickly deflated, however, when the three Balinese District Court judges refused to grant her lawyers more time to produce new witnesses. A distraught Schapelle was taken back to Kerobokan. Hutapea remained upbeat, saying he would take the matter to the High Court and seek leave for further witnesses to give evidence.

Two Qantas check-in staff gave evidence, taking the court through their job descriptions and both said they noticed nothing unusual about Schapelle's bag when she checked in. Hutapea pushed one of their heads into the marijuana bag saying 'you would smell this'. He then opened the bag and waved his arms around theatrically, demonstrating what a pungent aroma was emanating from the bag. Both check-in staff said they could not remember it and were relying on computerised records that indicated they had handled Schapelle's boogie-board bag early on the morning of October 8, 2004.

Qantas staff member Howard John Parr, 44, said he was a check-in agent, not security staff and Ricky Leigh Clark, 27, said he accepted Schapelle's boogie-board bag in the oversized luggage area but did not notice any smell of marijuana. Hutapea had the bag of marijuana weighed during August 3, 2005 and it weighed only 3.6kg (8lb)—making it half a kilogram (just over one pound) lighter, which meant that amount had gone missing. He jokingly accused the prosecutors of taking it. 'Is it possible... evidence disappeared just like that?' he said, accusing the Balinese police of failing in their investigation in this case.

Chief Judge Linton Sirait ordered the drugs be examined by police again. Faced with the day's setbacks, Hutapea criticised the Australian Justice Minister Chris Ellison's handling of the case, saying Canberra had not done enough to allow new witnesses to testify under immunity and that the Australian Government seemingly did not want Schapelle freed. Senator Ellison said he was worried by reports that a distressed Schapelle believed her Federal Government was not doing enough to help her.

To rub salt into the wound, it was revealed that High Court Chief Judge, I Gusti Made Lingga, had written to both Judge Sirait and Hutapea telling them that the defence plans to video-link testimony for some witnesses from Australia would be unacceptable. Senator Ellison said his office would write to the Bali High Court to support Hutapea in an application to have the case reopened with video link evidence from Australian witnesses such as Prisoner Paul.

Sadly, after rereading the last few paragraphs, it becomes painfully obvious just how little Hutapea had to work with at this hearing.

Nothing happened for several weeks and the matter dragged into late August 2005 and it became apparent there would not be any further hearing—just a decision from the Bali High Court on Schapelle's appeal. The three judges were due to make their decision by August 27, 2005 but one of the trio had to spend a week on 'judge's training' in Jakarta. I was told it was mandatory for this judge to do the refresher course and that would extend the appeal to September 30.

Hutapea told me that during the previous few weeks, he had staff members at his law firm researching marijuana cases in Indonesia and he could not understand how the court could have handed down a 20-year sentence for a marijuana offence.

'I have done some research and I have even found a case where a man had 161kg (355lb) of marijuana and he was sentenced to 10 years jail,' he said. 'From looking at court cases throughout Indonesia, involving quantities of marijuana similar to what was found in Ms Corby's bag, then she should have only been sentenced to three or four years.

'Of course we believe she is innocent and should be freed, but under the circumstances, I find that a 20-year sentence is extremely heavy and unprecedented in our country for marijuana. I am writing to the Supreme Court in Jakarta about the severity of this sentence in a case that many of us think should never have even reached the court stage.'

Around this time, a persistent rumour emerged in Bali, and then Australia, that Schapelle was going to get her sentence cut in half to 10 years. Who knows where it came from? It was picked up by the Australian media, which surprisingly led to Australian Foreign Minister Alexander Downer responding to it, saying he could not confirm whether it was true. 'There's a rumour that her sentence is to be halved by the Bali High Court but we have no way of confirming that at this stage,' he said.

Mr Downer's comments infuriated Hutapea. 'I am writing to your Foreign Affairs Minister, Alexander Downer to ask why he would publicly comment to what even he described as a rumour about Ms Corby's sentence being reduced,' he said. 'I can't understand why he would do this, because of course the judges will think we leaked the rumour, which we did not.'

Schapelle and her family were finding the wait exhausting and frustrating. Mercedes said on August 23, 2005: 'It just keeps hanging there over our heads. I know Schapelle gets very frustrated at times, but she will not go right down because she knows at some stage her innocence will win the day.'

At this time the number of Aussie citizens arrested in Bali over drug matters grew, with Adelaide-born Michelle Leslie, 24, arrested at a dance party with two ecstasy tablets in her handbag. An international model, Leslie sent the media into a total frenzy for weeks. Rosleigh said she understood perfectly what Leslie's family was going through following the model's arrest.

'I can't say much about her (Leslie's) case because I only know what I've seen on the Balinese media, but I can say that Schapelle is different to all those other Australians facing drug charges in Bali because she did not know the drugs were in her bag at all and she is totally innocent,' she said. 'I just hope those parents of that Adelaide girl aren't thinking that this will just go away, because it won't.' Leslie served a few months in prison before returning to Australia.

A lull fell over Schapelle's case as the days of September ticked by, with a result expected on September 30. The sentence reduction rumour continued to do the rounds to the point that I started to think about the old adage about no smoke without fire, but I kept my thoughts to myself and Elaine. Mercedes said she and Schapelle had been confident of freedom from the appeal, but that confidence had weakened as the weeks rolled on.

Only a few days before the appeal decision was due to be announced, Bali High Court Chief Judge Made Lingga had written to his superiors at the Supreme Court in Jakarta asking for a 30-day extension, which was automatically granted. Legal sources in Bali told me the extension was needed because there was an impasse, with one of the three judges believing Schapelle was innocent and there had to be consensus among the trio. Whether this was true or not will probably be never known, but it added to the frustration for Schapelle, her family and supporters. And that frustration welled over, with Mercedes writing to the Australian Government expressing her feelings that they had not done enough for Schapelle and that they had been too quiet about the state of Australian airports.

While the waiting dragged on it was Mercedes who next made the headlines when the spectre of evil returned to Bali with the second wave of suicide bomb blasts killing 26, including five Australians, on October 1, 2005.

More than 110 people were injured and Mercedes and her husband Wayan were in the thick of things, making repeated mercy dashes to the hospital, ferrying the injured and maimed to safety. Mercedes had been on her way to dinner with Wayan and Sydney documentary maker Janine Hosking when they saw people running out of Kuta Square. 'We didn't hear the explosion, we just saw everybody running and I have some first aid training, so we jumped out of the car and helped people,' she told me hours later by phone.

'I was in the first police truck and I was nursing an Indonesian woman who had half her face blown off, but later at the hospital I couldn't find her. There were a lot of shrapnel wounds and broken bones as well as burns, but mostly shrapnel wounds, and most of the Aussies I saw were going to make it.'

Suicide bombers had targeted restaurants in Kuta Square and at the popular Jimbaran Bay dining precinct, which was always packed with Balinese families as well as tourists. Ms Hosking told me that Mercedes had been magnificent. 'She was helping out where she could, calming people down, and after the year she has been through it was just incredible to see her in action,' she said. Rosleigh told me a few days later that the Balinese woman with half her face blown off had survived because of the quick actions of Mercedes.

'They are saying because Mercedes got her to hospital so fast, that is what saved her,' she said. She said the whole family was very proud of Mercedes and Wayan. 'Schapelle is very proud of her big sister, but she pleaded with me to stay off the streets and away from big restaurants and it's sad that it's come to this.'

Elaine and I arrived in Bali four days after the bombings and found an eerie, sombre mood pervading Kuta, whose normally teeming, bustling streets were almost empty. We went and looked at the one of the bomb sites—the burnt-out shell that had been the upmarket Raja Steak and Pasta Bar in the Matahari shopping complex—in the ritziest section of Kuta. The Balinese people, who are normally happy souls, looked very glum and some approached us on the street, apologising for what had happened.

The bombings were on everybody's minds in Kuta and as I sat with Rosleigh, Greg and Mick on the restaurant patio at the Kendi Mas Hotel, Rosleigh admitted the family had harboured fears of a terrorist attack at the court room during Schapelle's four-month trial earlier in the year.

'It was always on our minds the night before each court appearance,' she said. 'By the time we got into court and saw Schapelle, those thoughts went out of our minds and we only thought about her. They were no real reasons for us to have those fears. They were just there. I know Schapelle thought about it because she had nightmares about something happening.'

At Kerobokan, Elaine met Schapelle on October 6, 2005. Schapelle gasped as she looked at the photos of the latest bombing victims that displayed in the edition of the *Gold Coast Bulletin* which featured her sister as the 'Angel of Bali'.

'This is just awful,' said a visibly shaken Schapelle. She said police had come to the jail the day after the latest bombings to interrogate the convicted Bali bombers from the nightclub attack three years earlier.

'We did not know why they (the police) were here at first, but nothing's a secret in here for long and after they went to J Block where the bombers are kept, word soon got out about what had happened in Bali the night before.' Schapelle was very edgy on this visit and the suicide bombings had clearly spooked her. She was also struggling to come to terms with the fact that she had spent one year behind bars. I asked her if it felt like she'd been locked up for 12 months and she replied: 'Sometimes it doesn't, then other times it does and there are other days when it feels like I've been in here much longer.'

Sitting cross-legged on a mat in the visitors' area, she still looked alert and crisp.

'Nothing much has changed since you were last here,' she said, in reference to my visit in July. 'The best thing, I guess, is that we now have running water in the women's section thanks to the Red Cross, which means we don't have to fill our bucket every morning and only be allocated one bucket for the day.'

The water pump didn't last long on that occasion and is still a major issue for the female inmates in 2008. In October 2005, Schapelle's cell population had increased from 8 to 11. 'I have my little stove in front of the toilet area and there's just constant traffic the whole time,' she said. Support for her was still coming from all over the world and she said it helped keep her strong.

Our next visit, on October 11, 2005 was going well when the guards suddenly appeared early and started hustling us out of the visitors' area at 11.20am, well before the appointed time. We tried to argue, but they were adamant and Schapelle and the other prisoners were confused and had no idea what was going on either. Elaine and I were with Rosleigh and her youngest daughter Meleane and we all moved back into the main entrance area, where we were confronted by two rows of soldiers in full kit carrying automatic weapons at high point. It was quite frightening and we had no idea what was going on.

Outside the prison, three armoured personnel carriers were lined up in front of the jail and a large media pack had gathered. When we had arrived at Kerobokan, there had been no media or army personnel in sight. We asked some of the media what was going on and they told us the authorities were moving the Bali bombers out of Kerobokan. It was thought that the Balinese, angry at the latest suicide bombings, might storm the prison and the move came a day before a protest was planned outside the prison. But it was a strong reminder to us that Schapelle had no real control over her life, like any other prisoner in the Indonesian penal system.

The next day, October 12, 2005, we were all gathered at Kendi Mas when news broke around 2pm that Schapelle's sentence had been cut to 15 years. Mercedes asked Elaine and me to fetch Mick and Greg, who were having a beer at The Pub in a nearby street, because she was afraid the media knew Mick Corby was a regular at that bar. We raced around and told them to leave and Mick was reluctant to come until I told him why. I didn't feel it was my place to do so, but he insisted, so I told him of the five-year reduction and he just stopped on the street and said: 'So now we know it's 15 years. That totally sucks.' As we walked back to the hotel, he just kept repeating '15 years, 15 years'.

Back at the hotel, family members were tearful and irate as mobiles rang constantly with media reps wanting comment. Rosleigh blamed her daughter's predicament squarely on the Australian Government.

'I don't care what lip service they have peddled in the last 12 months to the Australian media, the bottom line is simply they have not done anything to really help Schapelle and they were in a position to really help,' she said.

'It's ironic to think there were Downer, Ellison and Keelty all at the memorial service (for the third anniversary of the first Bali bombing held that week), talking about great friendships with Indonesia and the truth is, they won't alter one bit their foreign policy with Indonesia to help an Australian. I want the people of Australia to be angry and upset like I am, and to put pressure on their Federal MPs. This is clearly political and Schapelle is being made a scapegoat for something she has not done. I've said it often, she is innocent and I will be bringing her home and it bloody well won't be in 14 years from now.'

This was now a major international issue as well, rather than just another court case over drugs. Relations between Indonesia and Australia had been strained—particularly if we look back over Australia's world-leading stance over East Timor.

Australian Government officials told me they considered the period from 2002 till the present as one of consolidating relations between the two countries at a government level.

During that period the relationship had to withstand terror-related issues, including the perceived lenient sentence of Indonesian cleric Abu Bakar Bashir, who served only 15 months in jail for his role in the first Bali bombing, illegal Indonesian fishing boats in Australian waters, Papuan asylum seekers as well as the Australian public's reaction to Schapelle's case and those of the Bali 9.

While understanding the Corbys' frustration and anger at what they saw as Australian Government inactivity, the responses by the Howard Government, given the bigger international picture, are in some ways understandable. The conclusion to the *Melbourne Age's* editorial the day after Schapelle's conviction in May 2005 struck the right chord with me.

'Whatever spin the Australian and Indonesian governments put on the present strengths of bilateral ties, the Corby case is yet another indication of just how fragile and shallow this relationship remains,' ran the editorial. 'At a government-to-government level, it is vulnerable to relatively minor jolts; and it was tested by somewhat erratic former President Soeharto, the deaths of the Australian journalists during the 1975 East Timor invasion and the 1999 intervention there by the Australian military. The Corby case is the latest in a succession of flash points. The test, for the Australian Government in particular, will be to stay the course in the face of populist outrage. Australians, meanwhile, need to be clear about the difference between sympathy for Corby's plight and the mutual respect a mature relationship between Australia and Indonesia demands.'

Rosleigh had been convinced her daughter was going to be released on appeal and she spent the rest of that day and night in her room, not reappearing until the next morning.

Mercedes was also visibly shaken and very angry at the Australian Government for what she saw as a lack of courage in not helping her sister. 'They say they cannot become involved in the Indonesian legal system, yet here they are pleading with the Indonesian Government not to allow a paltry sentence for Abu Bakar Bashir to be lessened,' she said.

'All we have asked for is a simple letter from someone in authority in that Government explaining the terrible situation in Australian airports with drug trafficking that has swept up my sister into this dreadful mess. Schapelle is innocent. I guess five years off is a small step in the right direction, but that's all it is—a bloody small step and it means we need to take giant step forward at the next appeal stage in Jakarta.'

The following day, Schapelle gave Rosleigh a long shopping list. 'I'll need these things now that I know I'm going to be here for a lot longer,' she said. It was a courageous reaction to the news that any hopes of freedom were on hold again until the third level of appeal. She kept asking 'when will my innocence really count?' and 'why can't we find who put these drugs in my bag?'

Schapelle was also concerned about her health the longer she stayed in Kerobokan, saying the past year had been the sickest of her life. On her shopping list was a spoon. Rosleigh had brought her one less than week ago and it had already been stolen.

'One of the girls in my cage explained to me that the heroin addicts used the spoon. I had no idea about such things because, contrary to what some people think about me, I honestly know very little about drugs.' Considering Mercedes had only told Schapelle about her sentence reduction that morning, she was remarkably composed. As Elaine and I got up to leave and Schapelle knew we were flying back to Australia that night, she said: 'I wish I was going with you. A reduction to 10 years would have been nice, but really I always knew I wouldn't be going before the appeal stage in Jakarta. I just have to stay tough in here and I will do that.'

Lawyer Erwin Siregar's message was upbeat—'the game is not yet over for Schapelle'. They lodged their appeal to the Supreme Court—Indonesia's highest court—on October 31, 2005, claiming lower court judges had failed to consider evidence that would free her. Prosecutors in Denpasar lodged their counter appeal, asking for the sentence to be life. Siregar said there was so much doubt in Schapelle's case and he remained confident of the outcome. But it would be very hard to wipe out 15 years in one appeal.

24.

Christmas in an overcrowded cell

NOVEMBER 2005 was notable for Schapelle because there were now 13 prisoners in Cell 7—a 4m x 3m box (13ft x 10ft) crammed with humanity. Schapelle's personal space was a miserly 0.92sqm (3ft) and Mercedes said when the women tried to sleep on their mattresses on the floor, they were touching shoulder to shoulder. 'It's disgusting, but there seems to be little we can do about it, but the people of Australia need to realise that conditions here are totally different from what you would find in Australian prisons,' she said.

Rosleigh said Schapelle didn't dwell on the cell conditions too much. 'But from little things that are said, you get the impression that life is pretty tough in there,' said Rosleigh.

A new scandal erupted on December 9, 2005, when the Melbourne *Herald Sun* reported that South Australian police had found photos of Schapelle Corby and a man in his 40s when they raided the man's Adelaide home. This Adelaide man had been charged, and would later be convicted, with smuggling marijuana from South Australia to Queensland. The article stated that the photo was taken before Schapelle's arrest and this led to broader media speculation that its discovery could see Schapelle getting a stiffer sentence.

It was all very damning stuff. Mercedes said Schapelle was adamant she had nothing to do with drugs and could not remember being photographed with a South Australian man in his 40s. She said Schapelle had never even been to South Australia. The South Australia police media unit would not confirm or deny the existence of any photos.

'It's disgusting these attacks are being made and Schapelle cannot defend herself,' she said. 'It is as though she has her arms tied behind her back and the media are taking free shots at her.' She said the newspaper report had errors in it.

'It said my father Michael was convicted of a marijuana offence in 1981, but the truth is he was fined $400 after marijuana was found at a party he was attending and no conviction was ever recorded against him, and we have the paperwork from the Queensland police to prove it.'

The article also stated that Schapelle brushed aside the hands of Balinese customs officer Gusti Winata or another unnamed officer when the 4.1kg (9lbs) of marijuana was uncovered in the unlocked boogie-board bag at Bali Airport. I searched the court transcripts for my report in the *Gold Coast Bulletin* and the transcripts showed that neither Winata nor anyone else was touched by Schapelle. The *Herald Sun* journalist, Keith Moor, who wrote the original story, rang me and asked if the Corby family would speak to him. I told him there was no chance under the circumstances.

He told me that Rosleigh was also in the photos and that she and Schapelle were dressed up as though they were going out to somewhere special. I told him I would pass on that information to Rosleigh and when I did by phone, a short time later, you could have heard a pin drop. Then Rosleigh started to wrack her brain about who took the photos and where they would have been taken. She told me that she didn't dress up ever and could not imagine the circumstances where that had happened. She spent the day working it all out, then she called me the following day, on December 12, 2005 and she was quite distraught, telling me she was responsible for her daughter being photographed with an alleged drug smuggler.

'I kept thinking we didn't know anyone in South Australia, but late in the day after talks with South Australian police, I remembered two men that approached me and Greg at the Secret Garden (a restaurant/bar in Kuta) during the trial and the more I think of it, it had to be them,' she said.

Rosleigh said Schapelle knew nothing of the men, who said their names were Mal and Dave, until she and Greg took them into Kerobokan to meet Schapelle in April or May 2005.

'Greg and I were having a drink in the Secret Garden when these two men came over and said they felt for us and supported Schapelle,' said Rosleigh. 'They seemed like a couple of nice Aussie battlers... Mal said he had an eleven-year-old granddaughter who felt for Schapelle and they asked if they could go to the prison and meet her. They wanted a photograph with Schapelle and they were going to get a disposable camera, but they didn't in the end, so Greg took the photos on his digital camera and then we got prints for them. Schapelle wrote a card for Mal's granddaughter. This was the only time Schapelle saw or had anything to do with these men. I'm so upset that I innocently took them to see Schapelle and one of them is involved in drugs and I know people will see that as sinister somehow, but we knew nothing about them and just thought they were being nice for supporting Schapelle. All I can do is tell the truth and this is the truth.'

Rosleigh then received a fax from South Australian Police

Commissioner Mal Hyde stating the photos 'did not appear to be in a prison setting'. That lit a fuse under Rosleigh and she headed off to Adelaide to get her hands on the photos, but she received knockbacks from both the South Australian police and the AFP, with both bodies stating she could not have access to the photos which were classed as evidence.

Then on December 16, 2005, Dave, who was not facing any charges and said he had first met Mal on the flight to Bali, handed his set of photos to the *Adelaide Advertiser*. 'He was concerned the whole thing was damaging Schapelle and the photos were exactly as I said they were, taken in the visitors' courtyard at Kerobokan,' said Rosleigh. She then took the photos to Bali to hose down some damaging media reports there by showing them to Bali prosecutor Ni Wayan Sinaryati.

Like so many other misleading incidents, there is no doubt this one harmed Schapelle, despite there being no wrongdoing by her at all. But this incident is the one that people most often mention to me in explaining their belief that Schapelle is guilty.

The main man in the photo, identified by Rosleigh as Mal, turned out to be a Malcolm McCauley, 60, who later told the *Adelaide Advertiser* that the message Schapelle wrote to his grand-daughter was: ' When you're old enough to travel the world, remember to lock your bags.'

McCauley told the *Advertiser* that the story surrounding the photos had been a 'beat up' and it had ripped his life apart. He said he required medical treatment for stress and had been ostracised by his family and friends. He was extradited to Queensland and later found guilty of drug importation and jailed.

While Rosleigh was in Adelaide, Schapelle joined the Bali 9 members for a Christmas party in Kerobokan on December 16, 2005. The 10 inmates, plus family members, got together for stuffed roast chicken, salads and an array of desserts including plum pudding, mince pies and gingerbread men, supplied by Sanur Deli owner Annie Sihombing. Mercedes and her family joined the party, held in a private room, and Michelle Stephens, the mother of drug mule Michael Stephens, dressed in Xmas garb and handed out 10 presents from under a Xmas tree she had bought into the jail. Scott Rush's parents Lee and Christine handed out party hats and had an Esky full of soft drinks. It was rare that all 10 Australian prisoners mixed together.

Christmas Day, 2005 was a Sunday, so normally there were no visitors but Mercedes received permission for a special Christmas Day visit. She went to the prison with her dad Mick, husband Wayan, her children Wayan junior and Nellie, plus other members of Wayan's family. She said the Christmas Day meal was a simple affair of ham and salad rolls with some delicacies from Bali Deli. 'It was simple and quiet and the only difference to last year was that we had Thai food then,' said Merc. After lunch, they joined Schapelle for a church service before she went back to her cell for her normal 4.30pm lock-down.

The end of 2005 found Schapelle unwell with an ear infection, flu and *mata merah*, that severe Indonesian version of conjunctivitis, which ended a year that was one of the worst for poor health in Schapelle's life. 'Just about everything that could go wrong did in 2005, but we have greater hopes for the New Year,' said Mercedes.

Those hopes, sadly, were quickly dashed.

A phone call early on January 19, 2006 from a colleague at Gold Coast Channel 9 *News* told me that a Channel 9 cameraman had filmed Schapelle's half brother James Kisina a few hours earlier, being taken into the Beenleigh Watchhouse, south of Brisbane, following his arrest for a home invasion earlier in the week. I couldn't believe it so I immediately rang Rosleigh's partner

Greg Martin and he confirmed that he had been on night shift and had come home to find Rosleigh's Loganlea house had been turned over by police.

Rosleigh was back in Bali. I agreed to meet Greg at Beenleigh Magistrates Court where James was appearing later that morning. I sat in on this case as a *Gold Coast Bulletin* reporter. James stood in the dock, dressed in a Queensland prison brown track suit, appearing stunned and confused by the events that had led to his arrest. He was charged with two counts of deprivation of liberty, two counts of assault occasioning actual bodily harm, one count of producing a dangerous drug, possessing a dangerous drug, possession of anything used in the commission of a crime and entering a dwelling with intent to commit an indictable offence. As an experienced police reporter, it was clear to me that the detectives hadn't missed anything—they'd thrown the book at him—and I didn't need to hear that the court was told police considered the charges to be serious. I knew for sure that James would be spending time behind bars.

The court was told the offences were carried out in Rochedale, south of Brisbane, in the early hours two days earlier. James had been arrested with two other men including his cousin, Shane John Tilyard, 19. Police alleged the three men, wearing balaclavas, broke into the house, tied up the occupants, a couple in their 20s, gagged the woman and struck the man with an iron bar. They allegedly stole $1000 and a quantity of marijuana, which was taken to Rosleigh's home where James lived.

Court appointed lawyer Stefan Simms told magistrate Peter Webber that James believed there were alleged drug dealers at the Rochedale address who may have information about, or may have somehow been involved in, the case of his sister, Schapelle. 'He's a young man who's acted emotionally, irrationally and it's clear he has a great love of his sister,' said Mr Simms. 'The

Schapelle Corby case has been going for some time and James has felt anger and frustration at what has happened to his sister, but until this incident he had not reacted at all. He is a young man who acted very emotively instead of taking whatever information he had to the proper authorities.'

Mr Simms said James had been unemployed since Christmas, but had been looking for work since ending a landscaping job. 'The police affidavit suggests he has been smoking cannabis, but there is no evidence of that,' said Mr Simms. 'It also suggests that he was suspected of being involved in drug trafficking with his sister, but again there is not a shred of evidence to support that.' Mr Simms said James had one matter on his record, which related to a 'minor melee' on the Gold Coast, and this charge was dealt with in the Southport Magistrates Court in April, 2005, with no conviction recorded. 'When I read the police statement on this matter, I expected to find my client would have a long history of previous matters, but that is not so. There was virtually nothing at all,' he said. 'He was extremely upset when I told him the press was at the court, and he immediately asked if this would have any effect on his sister's case,' he said. The magistrate denied bail and James was remanded in custody.

Greg and I spoke to Mr Simms outside the court. I was concerned that police had linked James to Schapelle in writing without any evidence at all and I knew the media would have a field day with that angle. Outside the court I relayed these feelings to an upset Mercedes by phone. She asked me if I would help her brother Michael get a good lawyer for James and I agreed to help. Michael had heard of a Gold Coast lawyer, Jason Jacobsen, and I knew of him and told Michael he had a good reputation. Later I called Mr Jacobsen and told him of my concerns with certain unsubstantiated comments in the police affidavit sworn by arresting officer Detective Sergeant Dean Godfrey. This included the claims about James' supposed links to the 'exportation of cannabis for which his sister received a 20-year imprisonment sentence.' The affidavit also claimed James had a 'propensity to commit offences' and had suffered from a 'lack of parental guidance'. I pointed out to Mr Jacobsen that the *Oxford Dictionary* defined propensity as a tendency or inclination and, as James had no previous convictions, only the one minor mention for affray, this statement was incorrect.

As for lacking parental guidance, James was now 18 and as far as the law was concerned, he was considered to be an adult, rendering parental guidance irrelevant. Mr Jacobsen agreed these three statements were of concern and said he would look at them as soon as possible. Needless to say, the media didn't miss them and by the time Mr Jacobsen had them removed from the affidavit, the damage was done, as was so often the case with the hapless Corbys.

Back in my office that afternoon, I was working on the court story and I was also fielding a number of phone calls from Corby supporters, when I took a call from an ABC radio producer asking me to comment on the news that Schapelle's sentence had boomeranged back to 20 years. I told her that could not be correct as the Supreme Court judges had only been appointed a few weeks earlier in Jakarta to hear the third and final appeal. Within minutes, other media were ringing me with the same news and I realised that this news was true.

The news had caught the family by surprise and a stunned Rosleigh and Mercedes had left the office of Bali lawyer Erwin Siregar shortly before 4.45pm Bali time on January 19, 2006 after being told the three appeal judges had made the decision to dismiss the defence application and accept the prosecution appeal of a return to the original sentence. The judges had made this decision a week earlier on January 12, 2006.

The family and supporters were shattered. A tearful Rosleigh, carrying bunch of flowers, arrived at Kerobokan the next morning with Mick and Wayan. Mick said his daughter was 'just a poor bloody kid who is innocent' but it was Wayan who really broke the family's silence telling me that Schapelle was angry, very upset and all involved were at a low point, but they were determined to continue the battle. 'Justice in Indonesia is not right, it is not balanced. We have people getting lighter sentences when they have had bigger quantities of drugs and many more serious drugs, not that we are saying Schapelle was carrying the marijuana anyway,' he said.

'The drugs were never tested—there were so many things wrong with the trial and appeal,' said Wayan. Michael Junior said the family would find a way to keep the battle for Schapelle's freedom alive.

Rosleigh told Channel Nine's *A Current Affair* that her youngest son's arrest was not linked to Schapelle's arrest and conviction in Bali. 'This has nothing to do with James or what he has done, she said. 'I love James very much... I'll deal with him when I get home.'

She also told me later that a young female had played a role in his actions by convincing him and his two mates that the couple whose home they invaded had something to do with the drugs found in Schapelle's boogie-board bag. This female disappeared after James' arrest and was not later prosecuted for her role in the crime. Rosleigh was adamant that what James had done was completely wrong but equally convinced the spectre of Schapelle's dire situation hung over his actions in this case.

Back in Indonesia, Hotman Hutapea bitterly complained that Schapelle's case was in ruins and said he might quit her legal team. He said the arrest of James Kisina had 'ruined' his attempt to free her and he hit out again at the Australian Government, accusing it of mishandling her case from the outset.

The Australian newspaper reported on January 24, 2006 that 'Queensland police admitted yesterday they did not have evidence to support allegations that Schapelle Corby's half brother was involved in the Bali drug run that put her in jail'. The senior detective who raised the link between Corby and her half brother James Sioeli Kisina admitted his claims did not meet the 'standard of proof' required to take action against Mr Kisina. This was reported on page seven, but in the five days after James was arrested, the damning—albeit totally unsubstantiated—allegations had been headlines news around the country. Queensland Police Commissioner Bob Atkinson ordered a review of all the allegations and Detective Sergeant Godfrey told *The Australian* that he had been asked to 'outline how I came to those conclusions'.

Despite that, the arrest of James on serious charges involving drugs was a watershed in the level of Australian support for Schapelle, a defining moment when many people who had supported her just dropped off her case, believing now that the drugs in her boogie-board bag were James' or, at the very least, he was involved with his sister in drug importation.

Even now, in 2008, I still get stopped in Gold Coast streets by people saying: 'James did it' or 'they were his drugs'. No-one has explained to me yet how a 17-year-old youth managed to get his hands on more than $30,000 worth of drugs. Schapelle has told me vehemently that she would not do jail time for anyone else, even a family member.

On January 24, 2006, only a few days after the bombshell appeal failure, Hotman Paris Hutapea announced he had quit Schapelle's case. In the last few weeks before the appeal decision I had trouble getting hold of him, which had not been the situation earlier, and it made me suspicious. When I finally reached him by phone after he announced he was heading for greener or wealthier pastures, I got the distinct impression that he was already distancing himself from the case.

I had heard that the case was political and the powers-that-be in Jakarta had said Schapelle's sentence had to go back to 20 years. That is supported by the fact that the appeal judges had not been in situ long enough to have reached any decision. I wonder if Hotman had been told in Jakarta that it was a *fait accompli* and he knew none of his usual pull would have any effect—he half hinted that to me in our last couple of conversations. In the end the case and its political implications were even bigger than he was.

He wished 'Corby every success' and disappeared from the scene as rapidly, and almost as dramatically, as he had arrived.

25.
Evidence destroyed

SHOTS were fired and one police officer was injured in a full blown riot at Kerobokan jail during the afternoon of January 31, 2006. Rioting prisoners rebelled against an attempted drugs raid, which followed a search on January 28, 2006 when police found 400 ecstasy tablets hidden under the floor of the prisoners' holding area. The police officer was badly injured when he was hit in the head by a rock hurled by a prisoner as police targeted three accommodation blocks. The prison is ruled to a large extent by Bali's main crime gang, Laskar Bali, which controls the flow of drugs in Kerobokan. No visitors were allowed in that afternoon and Schapelle remained safely in her cell. But it was an ugly reminder of the world she inhabited.

That same evening ABC TV's *7.30 Report* claimed across Australia that Mick Corby had been connected to a man allegedly involved in large scale marijuana cultivation. According to the TV report, Mick was a friend and neighbour of a man, known as Tony, being investigated by the AFP over a hydroponic marijuana growing operation. Mick had lived next door to Tony in the Queensland mining town of Middlemount in the mid-1990s, then they had been neighbours again in a more remote farming community. The ABC program claimed police found 5kg (11lb) of marijuana in vacuum-sealed bags, marijuana plants and cash on Tony's property in September 2004—a month before Schapelle's arrest. Rosleigh told me that Mick knew Tony and they had been friends and had worked at the same mine, but that Mick had not lived there for some time and the properties, while neighbouring, were large so it was not like being next door neighbours in suburbia. 'I've just had a gutful of people telling lies about us,' she said. 'I just feel sick and I'm going to get legal action this time.' She said Mick, over in Bali, was in a state of 'disbelief' about these latest drug claims.

'He hasn't lived on that property for more than two years because he was on the Gold Coast getting treatment for his cancer,' she said. 'If my neighbour is growing dope, does that mean I am too? That I'm a drug person? It's just more crap.'

Mick's neighbour Tony Lewis was later fined on drug offences, but was found to have had the drug for personal use. It was not hydroponic marijuana. But the most important fact was that no member of the Corby family was even mentioned in the court proceedings. It seemed to be a very long bow to try to link Mick Corby as a former neighbour to the Lewis prosecution.

It had become clear that every time Schapelle's case was mentioned in one media outlet, it had a ripple effect throughout most media, often with false statements being repeated several times. Many people appear out of the woodwork with an opinion anytime they hear the Corby name and they are encouraged to add their thoughts, whether they are rational or not. There have also been cases where Corby's name was put into a story to make it worth publishing or broadcasting, even if Schapelle's case had no bearing on that story.

No sooner had the Corbys drawn their collective breath, than Jodie Power again turned up in a women's magazine. In a report on February 13, 2006 the headline screamed at the reader:

'Schapelle's best friend: I feel betrayed.' Every time articles were written or spoken about Schapelle and or her family, there was someone who believed them and it all added to a media-driven image of Schapelle and her family.

While in Bali on another trip in March 2006, two articles in the *Jakarta Post* caught my eye. One reported that a solider was caught following a high speed car chase in South Jakarta with 199kg (437lb) of marijuana in his vehicle. The report said this amount of cannabis had a street value of US $37,894 which again reinforced the poor local value of the drugs found in Schapelle's boogie-board bag. The second article was about a former Jakarta prosecutor who was sentenced to 17 years jail for dealing in crystal methamphetamine, also known as ice or *shabu shabu*, as well as ecstasy tabs. He was also charged over owning unlicensed guns. Because of his former profession, the judges decided to make an example of him, with a 'very harsh' jail term of 17 years. It was clear that Schapelle had been treated harshly by the courts.

On March 17, 2006, the Bali police burnt the marijuana that had sent Schapelle to prison for 20 years. The media were invited to witness the fire and the drugs were piled on top of a drum beside the Denpasar District Court where Schapelle had been convicted.

This vital piece of evidence had never been tested to determine where it had originated.

There was little fuss apart from some dizziness among spectators after Chief Prosecutor I Ketut Arthuna, who led the case against Schapelle, poured petrol on the pile and set it alight. Watching on was Deputy Mayor Anak Agung Puspa Yoga with police chief Hari Dono Sukmanto and a small group of journalists and photographers.

Schapelle's now infamous boogie-board bag also went up in

flames, along with the board and her surf fins. Drugs from other cases were also incinerated and there were even bottles of illegal homemade beer added to the pyre.

Around the same time, an interesting court case was reported in Sydney's *Daily Telelgraph*. The Central Local Court heard how a Brisbane man became an innocent drug mule when 10kg (22lb) of cocaine was hidden in his luggage without his knowledge. The court was told he checked two bags onto a flight from Argentina on October 8, 2004, but when he landed he could not locate his bags. It was revealed that baggage handlers had been paid $300,000 to remove the bags in Sydney before Customs could inspect them. The tourist denied any knowledge of the drugs and was not charged with anything. In the same trial, a star witness, using the pseudonym Tom, told the court of his role as a principal in the cocaine smuggling syndicate, which had planned to import 200kg (440lbs) of the drug from South America using the same method with baggage handlers.

So there was evidence that sizeable quantities of drugs were being placed into the bags of innocent travellers and those bags were disappearing. But it was all too late for Schapelle and her lawyer to capitalise on it.

On April 6, 2006, a Sydney Federal MP told me that Schapelle might have been freed if the Federal Government had answered his questions about security at Sydney Airport 10 months earlier. MP John Murphy said two security cameras inside the baggage handling unit had been sabotaged on three occasions between October 2004 and May 2005. The cameras had been used to monitor baggage handlers as they sifted through baggage behind the airport's check-in area.

In answer to a question on notice to Federal Parliament, Justice Minister Chris Ellison confirmed the cameras had been moved. Mr Murphy had asked his original question to the Transport

Minister on May 11, 2005 after he received information about the cameras from a baggage handler.

'Those cameras were right where Schapelle's boogie-board would have been before it was loaded onto the flight to Denpasar and there has been a monumental injustice with her case that this information has not come out until now,' he said. 'Schapelle might have been out of jail now because this security breach, with two cameras sabotaged, should have created grave doubts in the Corby case and the Federal Government should have revealed all this during her trial in Bali in 2005.'

The Government later claimed the cameras were working on October 8, 2004. But given other drug smuggling and bag removing that was happening in the same section of the airport at the same time as Schapelle was there, there had to be doubt about the cameras functioning.

It was never properly explained why the government took so long to answer Mr Murphy's straightforward question and there is no doubt that an Australian Federal MP giving evidence in Schapelle's trial about security cameras being tampered with would have carried some weight. Of course, how much weight will never be known, but Schapelle should have been given the opportunity to use this witness at what would have been a critical stage in her original trial.

The possibility of a prisoner exchange program between Australia and Indonesia was raised on June 29, 2006, with the two governments in serious discussions.

The Corby family had discussed the issues with Schapelle and obviously there were pros and cons. Mercedes had asked me to check out whether Schapelle could get into the low-security Numinbah Correctional Centre which houses up to 25 low risk females in the picturesque Numinbah Valley in the Gold Coast hinterland, which would be close to the Corby family.

I established that it would be impossible for Schapelle to be eligible to be housed there before spending some years in a more secure Queensland facility. At the end of the day the family all told me that Schapelle would look at any transfer scheme when it happened and the decision would be hers alone. Naturally, the Indonesian authorities had to be prepared to put her forward for such a scheme anyway, it was not an automatic thing.

The next picture of Schapelle to hit the front pages came from a woman's magazine on July 8, 2006 which showed a new look Schapelle with short hair. The magazine article quoted former Kerobokan inmate Michelle Jolanda, who had served seven months for drug offences. She had been quick to sell her story and pictures to the magazine, having only been released in June 2006 and then deported to Singapore. The article showed a photo of Schapelle with a 'new look' and said she was with her sister Mercedes, but it was actually journalist Kathryn Bonella who was living in Bali while she worked on Schapelle's book *My Story*. They also used a photo of a small dog that the caption claimed died in the prison leaving Schapelle 'heartbroken.' In fact, Mercedes had taken her dog to the prison and left it with Schapelle to cheer her up and break the monotony. After a few weeks, she told me she took her dog home and I have since seen it there.

Jolanda claimed Schapelle's new hair style made her look 'boyish and butch' and she claimed Schapelle did the cutting herself, on impulse, with a pair of scissors and a razor. Then the article reported that: 'Schapelle dug a deep hole at the base of a tree near her cell, buried the shorn locks and uttered some words that sounded like she was delivering her hair back to nature.' Then Jolanda claimed that Schapelle dug it up an hour later after Renae Lawrence told her she should sell her shorn locks on eBay. She made yet another claim when she said Schapelle was terrified of becoming overweight in jail as she had a love of KFC food, which Mercedes delivered in plentiful supply. And finally she said that Schapelle 'developed a close relationship with an inmate that didn't meet with prison authorities' approval'.

Rosleigh said the lack of a shower coupled with Bali's constant humidity led Schapelle to cut her hair. 'To suggest it's a butch look is rubbish, it's simply a practical move for the Balinese climate, nothing more, nothing less,' said Rosleigh. 'The hair was disposed of in the normal way, there was no burying it or ritual words, that's all crap and any comment about selling it on eBay is also pure fantasy. It might have been mentioned as a joke, but no more than that.'

I didn't need Rosleigh or anyone else to refute the KFC story. I knew it was inaccurate because I have brought food for Schapelle myself and she mainly eats a vegetarian diet of fruit and vegetables, with chicken and pork on occasions. I have never seen her eat any junk food. I remember at one stage when she was sick during the trial, she asked Mercedes to buy a load of KFC for her numerous cellmates as a thank you for their help and sympathy during her illness. On the subject of boyfriends or special friends, she had told me once quite sharply in a 2005 visit that she didn't make real friends in a place like that. Rosleigh said simply that Schapelle had no relationships with anyone in Kerobokan and 'she spoke to people politely'.

'All Schapelle wants is to be left alone and given some space, but when other prisoners like this woman have cameras snuck into Kerobokan, it makes it hard,' she said.

On July 10, 2006, Schapelle spent her second birthday inside prison, turning 29. With her were Rosleigh and Mercedes and her children. In 2005, her birthday had fallen on a Sunday and no visitors were allowed on the Sabbath, so Schapelle was alone. 'She knows the rules, but she was very upset about it, so at least this time she'll have people who love her around her,' said Rosleigh.

Rosleigh took her daughter eight little patty cakes, because a big birthday cake would not work without a large knife. There was also sushi and presents like earrings and a new top. It was a quiet day with little to really celebrate.

Later in the same month, Schapelle's lawyers Erwin Siregar and Haposan Sihombing, visited Schapelle and gained her approval to lodge a final appeal to the Indonesian Supreme Court against her conviction. Schapelle approved a 19-page dossier for submission to the court.

Judicial reviews are rarely successful in Indonesia and their laws regulate that there are three reasons for a judicial review appeal, including new evidence, disparity of a decision made by judges and negligence by the judges. There was no new evidence, which was the strongest plank in past judicial reviews that had been successful.

Schapelle's lawyers submitted the application for a judicial review on August 11, 2006. The basis of their argument was that three levels of Indonesian courts had failed to prove Schapelle's guilt beyond reasonable doubt. They also argued she would not be so stupid to take the bag containing the marijuana into Bali knowing that Customs would check the bag. The document also used Hotman Hutapea's previous argument that Schapelle should never have been charged with, let alone be convicted of trafficking. If she had been tried for possession only, the maximum sentence would have been 10 years.

Rosleigh returned home from Bali in late July 2006, suffering from dengue fever, but the fever had not dulled her bluntness. She said the appeal was a chance to finally 'get to the truth'.

A tense looking Schapelle appeared in court for her final appeal on August 24, 2006, wearing a white shirt and black headscarf and battling through the massive media pack as usual. Mercedes yelled at photographers to 'get out' as they pushed for the best angle to shoot her sister. Inside, Schapelle grabbed Erwin Siregar's hand as camera flashes dazzled her. She turned to Mercedes and her brother Michael sitting in the court and said: 'This is ridiculous'.

Mr Siregar read the 19-page submission to the District Court, talking about 'mistakes at all judicial levels'.

'The ruling was made without adhering to evidence that appeared during hearing sessions,' he said. He said the absence of Schapelle's fingerprints on the plastic bag containing the drugs showed she had no knowledge of the marijuana and he added that the prosecution had failed to prove she was a drug dealer, drug user or part of a major drug running syndicate. The court hearing ended with a 10-day adjournment to allow her lawyers to try to obtain airport security footage in the hope that it showed the marijuana being planted in her bag. It was a forlorn hope, as Australian Customs had already stated that no such footage existed. The outcome of this judicial appeal was to be decided by the Supreme Court in Jakarta.

In October 2006, a woman's magazine claimed a romance existed between Schapelle and another prisoner, Tjin 'Eddy' Yu, a Chinese Indonesian from Medan who was serving four years for possession of ecstasy. The article, headlined 'Schapelle's secret prison lover', was full of innuendo about a prison romance and although Eddy was interviewed, he never directly claimed that he and Schapelle had sex. I met Eddy three times in mid 2005 and found him to be a pleasant guy with a good grasp of English. He had been working as a surf instructor in Bali when he was busted in Kuta and he met Schapelle in Polda when she was first locked up. Because of his good English, he helped her out and in return the Corbys looked after him with food, toiletries and the like.

He had no family or friends in Bali and while there was clearly a friendship, I saw no body language or signs of any romance. He could have seen Schapelle as a meal ticket, he helped her and was rewarded in kind. I know she was unhappy when he was transferred to Madura Island off the East Java Coast, because he'd helped her from the start, but Kerobokan is overcrowded and transfers are part of the daily fabric of the place.

While this story was doing the rounds, James Kisina was sentenced to four years jail on October 16, 2006 for his part in the home invasion. The then 19-year-old had served nine months on remand since his arrest, so he was eligible for release in November, which duly happened.

October 2006 also brought the good news that Mercedes was pregnant with her third child, though doctors at one stage feared she might miscarry because of the stress she was under, so she said she had kept the news within her family. But she was well and planned to return to Australia to have her baby.

In November, a woman's magazine alleged that Bali 9 ringleader and death row inmate Andrew Chan was Schapelle's new boyfriend. An unnamed former inmate is quoted in the article: 'They look like any other couple in love, hugging and kissing in the sunshine as they stroll to sit in a patch of shade...' It's hard to know what Andrew's very attractive and pleasant Balinese girlfriend would make of that. Schapelle and Andrew get along well, but as recently as February 2008, I have seen Andrew with his girlfriend and they have been an item for some time. The so-called former inmate claimed the 'cell block that houses Andrew and Kerobokan's other death row prisoners is in the middle of the women's jail'. Clearly this person has never been inside Kerobokan prison, because the tower that houses Andrew and the other death row prisoners is nowhere near the women's section.

In an interview in the *Bulletin* magazine, Schapelle talked about the rumours and lies about her. 'It's so ridiculous. If I did go out there would be photographs. I can't even walk around the jail without someone pointing a camera phone at me,' she said. And as for her retinue of lovers, she said the magazines simply made it up.

'It's complete fiction. None of it is true. I have never had a boyfriend or sex in here,' she said. 'Come on! This place is vile and disgusting. Where are we supposed to have done it... in the church toilet or the filthy visiting area? No way. I'm so embarrassed that people are reading this total crap about me. It's shattering. I feel so small. The whole nation reading degrading gossip—with the internet this gossip is worldwide. It crushes me and devastates me.'

However, her book *My Story* quickly went to the top of the bestseller list in Australia after its release late in 2006 and for the first time since her arrest, Schapelle was able to strike back. It gave her some satisfaction and that helped carry her through another depressing Christmas in prison.

Mercedes was involved in a Brisbane meeting with Federal Government officials shortly after she returned to Australia for her 2008 defamation case. Despite *My Story* being a bestseller, it appears that the Federal Government has taken any profits from the sale of the book.

Again the Corby family collectively had hopes that 2007 would bring some good news, but those hopes were quickly dashed early in the New Year.

26:
Friends and fallouts

MERCEDES and Wayan were enjoying life as best they could under the circumstances with their new child and second son Nyoman—the traditional Balinese name for the third born, a real cutie who had curly hair inherited from his granddad, Michael Corby. It had not been their intention to live in Bali, they had planned to spend a few months there in 2005 so their then two children could get a taste of Balinese family and culture before Wayan junior started primary school on the Gold Coast in 2006. That plan went out the window after Schapelle's arrest and they are now living in Bali indefinitely.

The *Melbourne Age* and *Sydney Morning Herald* announced categorically on January 2, 2007 that Schapelle was to be moved from Kerobokan to Sukun Women's Prison in the East Java city of Malang. It was something Schapelle had long feared—to be taken from Kerobokan in darkness and her sister arriving later to find her gone to some remote prison.

The report quoted Kerobokan Prison Governor Ilham Djaya as saying the move for Schapelle must go ahead because of overcrowding, explaining that Kerobokan had room for only 340 prisoners, but housed almost 900.

Mercedes scoffed at the report, telling me that Schapelle

would not be moved while the judicial review was pending and that she would remain in Kerobokan anyway because she had family living in Bali. This proved to be the case.

That drama lasted a few days, then it vanished into the ether. All was quiet until early February, 2007 when a producer from Channel Seven's *Today Tonight* (TT) rang me, wanting to get in touch with Mercedes. I rang Mercedes and found she was quite agitated; she had already had contact with TT and was certain whatever they were planning, it might involve Jodie Power, Ron Bakir and maybe Robin Tampoe. She kept wondering what was going to air but she had refused to appear on the program.

A media release arrived at the *Gold Coast Bulletin* on Saturday, February 10, 2007, headed 'Exclusive: Finally the truth about Schapelle'. This was inaccurate to begin with because the segments were almost exclusively about Mercedes and, to a lesser extent, Rosleigh. The press release claimed TT was presenting 'an unprecedented insight into the family of convicted drug smuggler Schapelle Corby in an exclusive interview with a close family friend set to blow the whistle on the entire Corby clan, screening on Monday night (February 12, 6.30pm) on Seven'.

This was the first night of ratings for 2007, with TT desperate to steal a march on arch rival, *A Current Affair* (ACA). The release continued: 'Last year, Jodie and Mercedes had a falling out and now Jodie is speaking out to clear her conscience and to reveal the truth about the tight-knit Corby family.'

Justifying her decision to finally break her silence, Jodie was reported in the release as saying: 'You know, she (Mercedes) was my best friend for that long, those things that she told me, I shouldn't be telling anyone, but she's hurt too many people now.'

The first program was on February 12. It focussed entirely on Jodie's allegations about the family. Jodie claimed Mercedes smoked marijuana, which in itself was not a major revelation. Mercedes admitted that she, like many other Australians, had tried grass in her youth.

Jodie also claimed Mercedes took marijuana to Bali and sold it. That does not fit in with the Mercedes I have come to know and I have spent weeks in the company of Mercedes and other family members. I have only seen Mercedes drink on a few occasions, and then very little, and I have never seen her badly affected by alcohol or any other substance and yet during this period she was under the most intense pressure of her life, pressure that would have driven many to strong drink or similar. Jodie claimed on the program that many more people knew the truth about the Corbys and she repeatedly implored them to come forward. One anonymous guy claiming to be an old school mate of Schapelle's was interviewed, claiming he partied with her, smoking dope. No-one else has since come forward.

The Corbys were interviewed on *A Current Affair* but it became tit-for-tat accusations and counter-accusations, including duelling lie detector experts.

The program was broadcast with 2.6 million viewers on the Monday night, and 2.2 million on Tuesday. Both shows ran out of steam by Wednesday, with a lot of replays, but *Today Tonight* still had 1.385 million viewers on the third night.

Jodie's ex-husband, Michael appeared on *ACA* and refuted Jodie's version of events. Jodie's mum Margaret made accusations about Mercedes and drugs on *TT*, then the following day contacted *ACA* and told them Mercedes and her family were not bad people. Vasu Rasiah also appeared.

Jodie made further claims: that she was asked by Mercedes to water cannabis plants at Mick Corby's property, that Rosleigh and the family sold drugs from the Southport fish and chip shop. *TT* broadcast an anonymous Centrelink worker, with their face blacked out, saying that Schapelle had visited the branch where she worked to collect her disability pension which had been issued for 'drug related psychological problems'.

During the early interviews I did with Mick Corby in October, 2004, he showed me a letter from Centrelink saying that Schapelle was entitled to a carer's allowance because she was looking after him, following his diagnosis with terminal cancer. He showed me this as a way of demonstrating what a good daughter she was.

Jodie was paid a sum of money for her story and she was kept in a secret off-shore hideaway in Fiji, thenVanuatu, for two weeks. Later, *TT* sent her on a skiing holiday to Canada with her children.

On the night of the first show, a clearly upset Mercedes sent me an email denying each and every one of the accusations made by Jodie.

Rosleigh was outraged and the only time I remember her laughing was when she said to me could I believe Mick Corby growing and maintaining a marijuana crop? I had to laugh with her, because the thought was ludicrous. If you knew Mick, though he was marvellous guy, the likelihood of him growing anything at all was next to none.

Each time there was an attack on a Corby, an untruth or half truth or even a rumour printed, broadcast or placed on the internet where they are absolutely no checks and balances, there was a negative impact on Schapelle and her situation.

The Corbys' long run as headline magnets continued within weeks of the *TT* program. Mercedes had come home from Bali because Mick's health had deteriorated. Elaine and I had been to see Mick in a Tweed Heads Hospital and for a while it looked like the end was near—when we saw him he was having trouble hearing and appeared to be very ill, but he rallied. Despite her Dad's condition, Mercedes had begun to relax a bit and she was trying to put the Jodie Power interview behind her.

Today Tonight then broadcast a program showing photos of Schapelle outside the prison, suggesting she could come and go as she pleased.

One of the photos I recognised on the program was one showing Schapelle and Mercedes at a Balinese beach, taken in November, 2004—six months before Schapelle's conviction. I was shown the photo by Schapelle's then lawyer Lily Lubis in her office in Sanur during an interview in May 2005, just before the verdict.

The only difference with the photo shown on TV was that Lubis and a police officer called Gunadi had been cropped out of the image. The photograph had been snapped when Schapelle was taken from Kerobokan, supervised by her lawyer and the police officer, to be formally photographed by police, and Lubis arranged for a lunch with Mercedes. She had organised for the group to go to a resort that was either closed or yet to open and Schapelle had enjoyed her lunch. Lubis had asked me not to report the incident as it should not have happened. In those days, prisoners could get out of Kerobokan for a day, but Ilham Djaya stopped those practices when he took over as Kerobokan Prison Governor. He told me categorically, there was 'no way Ms Corby was being released to go the beach or anywhere else'.

Rosleigh confirmed that the photo was taken on November 28, 2004. 'Mercedes gave the photo to Lily (Lubis) because Lily was in it, and we thought no more of it since then,' she said. She said the video footage aired on TT showing Schapelle with short hair was taken on Wednesday, February 28, 2007. 'On that day she was taken outside the prison to a dentist and Australian Consular official Brian Diamond followed the prison vehicle in his vehicle,' she said.

'It is the first time Schapelle has been taken to a dentist, for a 45-minute visit, with two guards. It's just crazy to think Schapelle is going to nightclubs and the beach. These rumours have been around Australia for ages now and we have always said that if it really happened, she would quickly be photographed by someone. If the television companies put as much effort into finding out who put the drugs in Schapelle's bag, she would be home by now.'

Before March, 2007 was over there was a legal battle looming over nearly $280,000 in funds from Schapelle's book sales and magazine interviews frozen by the Queensland Court of Appeal. On March 27, 2007, the Court of Appeal released suppression orders it made on March 2, that temporarily stopped the family spending $267,750 from the publication of Schapelle's memoirs, *My Story*. Also frozen was $15,000 intended for Mercedes for an exclusive *New Idea* article based on excerpts from 'Schapelle's jail diary'.

Rosleigh said the Australian Government was quick to tax the monies received from the book. 'They didn't miss out on the tax at all,' she said. 'All along the Australian Government has said they cannot interfere with Schapelle's case in Bali and now they are trying to interfere with us in Bali. The book sold in New Zealand, but their government is not trying to take any money.' She said the money would be earmarked for Schapelle's on-going legal costs, which are considerable.

Mercedes began legal action for defamation against the Seven Network and others in the New South Wales Supreme Court on April 2, 2007. Her Sydney lawyer Bill Kalantzis said unspecified damages were sought over the program's allegations to the effect that Mercedes Corby was knowingly involved in the Schapelle Corby drug importation, that she had sold drugs, that she had imported drugs to Bali and that she interfered with her sister's defence, costing her the chance of acquittal.

The court documents filed by Mercedes Corby asserted that all the allegations were false. The defendants included Channel Seven, *Today Tonight* presenter Anna Coren, reporter Bryan Seymour and Jodie Power, who made the allegations. Rosleigh launched her separate defamation case against the Seven Network in June 2007, with unspecified damages. Both told me they wanted 'their day in court'.

On May 15, 2007 Schapelle shared a joke with Indonesian Justice Minister Andi Mattalatta while he inspected Kerobokan—and she surprised everyone with her good grasp of Bahasa Indonesian, conversing with the Minister and prison governor in their language about her book, her time behind bars and her desire to return home. Asked about conditions in the prison, Schapelle told Mr Mattalatta: 'I want to get out of here soon, please sir.' He did not reply.

Throughout the Corby case, the bizarre had frequently appeared and June, 2007 proved to be no different, with both the Indonesian National Institute for Drug Abuse and National Narcotics Bureau reported in the press that it was considering the legalisation of marijuana so good use could be made of the benefits. National Narcotics Agency drug expert Tomi Harjatno was quoted in the English-language *Jakarta Post* on June 5, 2007 as saying that 'all this time we only emphasise the bad effects of marijuana. But people in Aceh (a province on the island of Sumatra) are using marijuana in their food recipes,' he said.

Schapelle's lawyer Erwin Siregar told me it was well known that marijuana formed part of the diet in Aceh. 'I am from Sumatra and that has been the case for quite awhile,' he told me. He said the fact that government agencies were talking about cannabis legalisation could only help Schapelle. Mr Siregar said the statements from the two influential agencies had been widely reported in the Indonesian media.

'I hope the three judges who are doing Corby's judicial review have seen them, even the fact the legislation is being openly discussed could help get a sentence reduction for her,' he said.

July 10, 2007 marked a sad milestone for Schapelle with her 30th birthday and her third inside the jail. Mercedes, Wayan and their three kids made the oft-repeated journey to Kerobokan, carrying gifts including a CD and clothes, chocolate cake, flowers and sushi. Schapelle told her sister she still felt 27, and that she would stay 27 years old until her release. She was depressed and upset, but she put on a brave face for her nephews and niece as they sat on the floor of the visitors' area.

There was more depression for Schapelle the following month when she missed out on a possible three-month sentence remission after being caught in her cell talking on a mobile phone. Schapelle apologised for breaking prison rules as mobile phones are considered to be contraband.

But it didn't go unnoticed in Australia that six men involved in the 2002 Bali bombing which had killed 202 people had their sentences cut by five months. Those who received remissions were serving between eight and 18 years for offences ranging from being bomb planners to sheltering key bombers after the attack.

Suddenly having a mobile phone in jail seemed very trivial.

27.
Mick Corby
passes away

A PHONE call to me at my office in early October 2007 tipped me that there was a case coming up in the Southport Magistrates Court connected to the Corbys that I would be interested in. I discovered that the Commonwealth was prosecuting a Centrelink worker over her comments on the Channel Seven program *Today Tonight* which had included the Jodie Power interview in February, 2007. In that show the worker had her face blacked out. After this person had appeared, Mercedes had contacted Centrelink trying to get Schapelle's file, but it had proved to be impossible without Schapelle's direct involvement.

I had also contacted Centrelink and had been told that an internal investigation was being carried out and that if the person who appeared on *Today Tonight* turned out to be a Centrelink employee, they would be prosecuted under Federal laws. But as the months rolled on, we forgot about it and moved on to other matters. Now Rosleigh and I agreed to meet at the Southport court complex, which services the Gold Coast region, for the afternoon hearing.

Rosleigh and her youngest daughter Meleane arrived at the

court and we sat at the back, wondering who in the court was the Centrelink employee. Natalie Pearson, 24, stood before Magistrate Terry Duroux and pleaded guilty to unlawfully communicating private information about a pension application made by Ms Corby shortly before she was arrested in Bali on October 8, 2004.

Commonwealth prosecutor Heather Cunningham told the court that Pearson had been employed at Centrelink's Palm Beach office and dealt with Ms Corby there in September 2004. 'On February 15 (2007), she appeared on (Channel Seven's) *Today Tonight* where she said she had seen Schapelle Corby's medical record and that it related to drug addiction and depression,' she said. She said Pearson admitted in a record of interview with AFP officers on March 23, 2007 that she had not seen any medical record of Ms Corby but had heard talk among other staff in the tea room that her medical records must be drug related after Ms Corby was arrested in Bali.

Outside the court, Rosleigh said she felt a little strange with her legs weak and I told her to sit down for a minute before facing the media outside the courthouse. I knew what she was feeling— it was the first time since Schapelle's arrest that the Corbys had gained a real victory and it had overwhelmed Rosleigh.

In December 2007, an ABC reporter contacted me, wanting to use me as a go between with the Corbys for a story they were working on for their evening radio program *PM*. It went to air on December 7 2007, with claims they had obtained a crime intelligence report from the Queensland Police Service. From the start I doubted this as they are very hard to get hold of and most police would be extremely loathe to hand them over to journalists. I could not get hold of any Queensland Police crime intelligence reports through the Freedom of Information Act.

The ABC claimed they did sight a report from a 49-year-old

woman who claimed to have information about a drug running operation between Brisbane and Bali happening a number of times a year on commercial flights. She claimed the men took amphetamines in false bottomed suitcases and used false passports. She said the four men were 'associates' of Schapelle. The program said that this woman had given police information that had led to a successful raid on a property near Gladstone where marijuana was found.

This was an old story about a marijuana bust on a property owned by Tony Lewis that neighboured Mick Corby's property, which had first emerged in February 2006.

Mercedes said that without the ABC naming the four people who were supposedly known to Schapelle, they couldn't take legal action. She had asked Queensland police about the so-called intelligence report and had been told they could not establish its existence. Senior Queensland police told me the same thing and they also said categorically that intelligence reports are always followed up and if there is a shred of credence to them, then those named in them are invariably interviewed. Not only have no charges come out of this so called report to police, but no-one connected to Schapelle and her family have ever been spoken to by police over this matter. This report was claimed to have been made in September 2004, and the timing is so 'perfect'—just a few weeks before Schapelle's arrest.

The next morning the print media followed the story as though it was a new story, which was not strictly correct.

This was yet another example in a long line of reports from various media outlets that could not be taken seriously. But to claim it was another 'piece in the puzzle' surrounding Schapelle, is hot air. If you believed any of this report, the Queensland police had been in possession of this intelligence for three years and three months and taken no action, which showed how important it was considered by police—if in fact it ever existed.

The media attention weighed heavily on Mick Corby. He had well outlasted his original diagnosis of six months, but the last few years of his life were filled with pain and frustration. This was double edged—the pain and frustration from the cancer itself and his seriously deteriorating hearing, which was seen in TV interviews, making him look foolish and even aggressive, when he was simply trying to hear. Shouting and speaking too loud is a classic deafness trait.

Mick's deafness and other health issues were never explained in any of the television interviews—many of which were made by people who knew the full extent of his problems. He also felt extreme pain and frustration at Schapelle's desperate plight and his inability to do anything about it; then as the months rolled by, he was angry and upset when he was falsely portrayed as a drug dealer and smuggler.

I had spoken to Mick for hours, often in Bali, and he forever questioned how this had happened to one of his beloved children and how the family's name had been dragged through the mud several times.

He moaned about his health and towards the end was deeply saddened by the fact that he could not return to Bali to see Schapelle for one last time.

Schapelle had been at one of her lowest ebbs in December 2007 as she faced her fourth Christmas in jail, according to Mercedes. The tedium of prison life had weighed heavily on her at that stage, but Mercedes said she brightened up when Rosleigh arrived just before Christmas. However, life was slipping away from Mick when Mercedes joined the family at Loganlea early in 2008 and finally Mick was taken to hospital in Brisbane. He lost his long battle with cancer on January 17, 2008. I offered our condolences to the family and broke the news in the *Gold Coast Bulletin*.

The next day Mercedes told the *Daily Telegraph Online* that 'Schapelle had been told the news about our dad's death and is very distraught'.

'She's devastated that she's been unable to see her dad for more than 18 months,' she said. 'She's been desperately hoping he'd get to make one last visit but he was too sick to travel. Our dad was a beautiful hearted man, generous and a loving father who lived for us three kids—Michael, Schapelle and me. He devoted his life to us and his three grandchildren. Before he got too sick he spent months in Bali with Schapelle and me. He would do anything for us. He struggled with prostate cancer for four years and during the past three has also had to endure humiliating rumours and lies about himself and his family in the press, which hurt him a lot. He was a very intelligent, hardworking, caring and honest man who had suffered greatly from pain. All his friends and family will miss him greatly. We hope he is now at peace.'

Rosleigh invited Elaine and me to the funeral, hoping it would not become another media circus. It was held at the Newhaven Funerals Crematorium and Memorial Gardens in Stapylton, south of Brisbane at midday on January 22 and it turned out to be a memorable, moving and lovely service, completely free of working media.

The service began with a selection of gramophone music because Mick was a collector of old gramophones and records, and then we heard from his sister Julianne about Mick's early days, his intelligence and how he played word games with his three kids to make them think. There were flowers from Schapelle, reminiscences from a fellow miner and generally there was a lot of love in that chapel. The Rolling Stones song, 'Little Red Rooster' closed the service and everyone went to a nearby pub, the Gem Hotel for light refreshments. There, Elaine and

I expressed the same thought we'd had during the service—that we wished many Australians could have seen this service because they would have seen a very close and loving family that we were proud to know.

Many people have asked me why the Corbys have shouted and sworn and carried on like they have at times. What people have to realise is that this is a family watching things happen to one of their own, having no control over anything to do with these proceedings and all along knowing Schapelle is innocent. Just picture yourself in that position constantly for a number of years and ask yourself how you would react.

The biggest shock at the funeral was to see how much Rosleigh's partner Greg Martin had deteriorated in his losing battle with terminal cancer. He was very thin, looked years older and was walking stiffly with the aid of a walking stick.

I arrived back in Bali on my sixth trip since Schapelle's arrest in early February 2008 to find Schapelle was back on the front pages of the Balinese papers (and prominently displayed in the news in Australia), but this time for the most innocuous of reasons. She and Renae Lawrence were the first prisoners to use a public phone installed in Kerobokan prison for the inmates to use. Schapelle spoke to the media of her pleasure at being able to use the phone to call her family. I had been a bit unsure about how I would find Schapelle so soon after Mick's death and I was pleasantly surprised. I went into the visitors' area ahead of Mercedes and Schapelle, who had just had a visit from her lawyers, was standing near the entrance.

I was amazed at how well she looked, her demeanour and attitude were great and it proved to me once again just how strong she can be. Family members have told me that some days she would not even leave her cell to see Mercedes, other days she would come out to the visitors' area and scream at her sister. These mood swings were clearly enormous, but that was totally understandable given her circumstances.

Professor Paul Wilson, Chair of Criminology and a Forensic Psychologist at Bond University in Queensland, Australia, met Schapelle in Kerobokan prison during her trial and then gave evidence about her character. He told me that in his experience with foreign prisoners in Asian jails (and he has interviewed a lot specially in Thailand) that they sink easily into depression. 'This is understandable with different food, the majority of other prisoners and prison guards who treat them as second rate, and the physical deprivations that you don't usually find in Australian prisons,' he said.

'Those who survive the best try and find work to do where work is possible. As far as I know Indonesian prisons don't provide much work and if Schapelle is not physically and mentally active any depression will just increase.'

However the Schapelle I saw in February 2008 was just a delight and she genuinely made me laugh at a number of things she said. Many Australians and people of other nationalities are still writing to her and sending her gifts. She showed me a pair of wool-lined boots some well-meaning person had sent— this person clearly had no idea of the steamy, tropical Balinese climate. She then pulled out a woollen poncho that would have been useful in a Melbourne or Hobart winter but was completely useless in Bali.

She told me tongue-in-cheek how she couldn't resist ponchos and had to order them every time she saw them in magazines. I told her that her image was forever damaged, especially coming on top of the news that she liked some country music and I would now think of her as a poncho-wearing country music nut. We all laughed and then she put the poncho on, began singing a country song, changing the lyrics to sing about her situation in prison. It was just lovely and for a second or two you forgot where you were.

But that feeling never lasts long in Kerobokan. Maybe she was just putting on an act for my benefit but even that takes some doing.

To see any of the Australian prisoners in Kerobokan now you have to be on an approved list and one journalist had written that it was because there were 'suggestions' Schapelle was taking money from tourists in exchange for being photographed with her. Anyone who knows Schapelle would just laugh this off as being photographed in the jail is one of her strongest pet hates. But maybe the list will keep the wannabes and hangers-on away from Schapelle in future. I was buoyed by my short trip, but that was tempered by the fact Rosleigh and Greg went to Bali within a few days of my return. Greg had decided he had to go quickly as his strength was waning rapidly and his trip was very emotional, with Schapelle shocked at his appearance and state of health.

The question of a prisoner exchange between Indonesia and Australia came back into the media on March 3, 2008 with news that Home Affairs Minister Bob Debus had held high level talks in Jakarta aimed at finalising a prisoner transfer treaty, which had languished over the previous 18 months. Media outlets even had Schapelle and some of the Bali 9 home within the year.

The excitement was short-lived with Indonesian Justice Department spokesman Kolier Haryanto saying there were still eight sticking points in the negotiations, one of them being that Indonesia wanted the Australian prisoners to serve two-thirds of their sentence before being eligible for transfer. This would mean that Schapelle would have to spend another nine years behind Indonesian bars.

As Brisbane-based prisoner advocate Kay Danes rightfully

points out, in all prisoner exchange treaties, for the prisoner to be selected for the program, he or she has to show they are worthy of such a privilege by showing considerable remorse for the crime they have committed and this would mean an admission of guilt, which would seem to be a most unlikely scenario in Schapelle's case, given her relentless protestations of innocence.

Mercedes and her three children were now back living near Brisbane with Rosleigh, with the two oldest children enrolled in school there. Mercedes told me that she had been concerned for some time that time that their English was not strong enough and they were learning more Mandarin than English in their school in Bali. Mercedes said she also wanted to help Rosleigh look after Greg, who now needed constant care.

This plan left Wayan and Michael living in Bali to look after Schapelle and, while it saddened Mercedes and Wayan to be apart, it was the only practical solution for that time.

Yet again we saw the flow-on effect on other members of her family of the incarceration of an innocent woman. Mercedes just shrugged that off and got on with caring for her three kids and helping her Mum.

28.
One step forward, two steps back

ON March 3, 2008 a Channel Nine program, *A Current Affair,* claimed that a Brisbane woman had snapped photos of Schapelle and Mercedes dining at a kebab restaurant in Kuta in February 2008. I had seen Schapelle in early February and her hair was shoulder length, while the woman in the photo had hair halfway down her back. Also, the woman in the photo was very thin and would have been more than 170cm tall. Schapelle is short, not as thin as the woman in the photo and is 159cm tall. The other woman bore absolutely no resemblance to Mercedes at all, plus she was blond and Mercedes had not been blond for almost two years.

Bali-based journalist Cindy Wockner caught up with Schapelle in Kerobokan Prison the following week when the media were inside during a tour of the prison by Indonesian Director-General of Prisons Untung Sugiyono. Schapelle told Mr Sugiyono that she had not been outside the prison except when she went to the dentist on three occasions under guard. She blamed people who 'want to make money'. Prison Governor Ilham Djaya was reported to be incensed by the 'dining out' claims, saying it was impossible for prisoners to leave Kerobokan for such things as dinner.

Then came some devastating news for Schapelle. Still hoping for a ray of hope in her legal battle to get a release from Kerobokan, it was revealed that Schapelle had lost her final appeal in another court in Indonesia. The decision came 18 months after the appeal hearing in the Denpasar District Court and it was unanimously made by three Supreme Court judges in Jakarta on the morning of March 28, 2008.

Indonesian Supreme Court spokesman Nurhadi said the judges wanted to send a strong message to other drug offenders in Indonesia. 'One of (the reasons) could be to create a deterrence effect for other perpetrators,' he said. The judgment said the judges involved in the original case and subsequent appeals had not erred in their earlier sentencing. This meant that they did not feel that Schapelle had been wrongfully found guilty on a trafficking charge that had never been investigated.

I rang Schapelle's lawyer Erwin Siregar and he said he was 'devastated'.

'It's unfair. I just can't believe it. I was very hopeful of a sentence reduction,' he told me. 'I just don't know what to say. I can't believe it.'

Schapelle was inconsolable in the prison and Rosleigh and Mercedes were uncontactable for the next few days. But by April 2, 2008, their attention was firmly on Ros' partner Greg Martin who was dying. Rosleigh had a houseful of people, with Greg's children and his elderly mother keeping a bedside vigil.

A few days before his death, Rosleigh was sitting with Greg when the phone rang and it was Schapelle calling from the new public phone in the prison. Rosleigh told Schapelle that the end was near for Greg, who hadn't spoken for a few days. Rosleigh passed the phone to Greg and told him it was Schapelle. She said he suddenly broke his silence and asked Schapelle if she was coming home soon and she replied in the positive. Greg's face lit up and he spoke lucidly for about two minutes. He never really spoke again, but died on Friday, April 4, 2008, happy in the sadly mistaken belief that Schapelle would be home soon.

After Greg's death, Rosleigh was understandably depressed and downhearted. Greg had been a source of constant support for Rosleigh and the others during the entire time following Schapelle's arrest and he would be sorely missed. His service was at the same venue as Michael's had been only a few months earlier. The pair had become good mates in the past few years and in their declining months under the roof of Ros' home in Loganlea, they would share a port or two in the wee small hours when the pain became too much for them to sleep. Coming so soon after the news of the final appeal failure, Schapelle was totally beside herself and kept to herself in the prison.

The Corbys pay for Schapelle's costs in Kerobokan jail, despite a newspaper report on April 2, 2008 which claimed she was one of 50 Australians in overseas jails who have shared taxpayer-funded loans to buy personal necessities. This was simply not correct.

With the appeal denied, things were looking very bleak for Schapelle. However, one ray of hope emerged on April 22, 2008 at the changing over of Kerobokan Prison governors. Outgoing Governor Ilham Djaya described Schapelle as a 'very good' prisoner and said she could be up for a prison job. This meant that it could slice years off her sentence. He said she had attained the rank of *Tamping* (pronounced *tumping*), where she leads a small group of prisoners, and that this would see as much as five months per year off her sentence. Then she could be promoted to the important role and higher rank of *Pemuka*, who is a leading prisoner that oversees the *Tampings*.

Mr Djaya said that if Schapelle made the rank of *Pemuka*, she would be eligible for a massive and unbelievable cut of up to 11 months off her sentence each year. For Schapelle, just to know this route was even available to prisoners was encouraging. 'Corby has a job to gather handicrafts from prisoners, like from sewing class and knitting class; she has learned everything,' said Mr Djaya. Given his encouraging words, it was sad for Schapelle that this was his last day, but if she makes the same impression on the new Governor, Yon Suharyono, in the same way, maybe there will be some light at the end of the tunnel.

On May 29, 2008, a four-person jury found that Channel Seven had defamed Mercedes Corby—with a total of 28 defamatory meanings delivered in three *Today Tonight* programs and a television news story in February 2007. The jury found only one of the seven defamatory meanings that Channel Seven and its co-defendants defended was true—that Mercedes had been guilty of possessing marijuana.

As she walked from the court with her team—Stuart Littlemore QC, Sue Chrysanthou and Bill Kalantzis—Mercedes said: 'I'm really happy, I've still got more to do. I am really happy with the outcome. It's been difficult but thanks to the great legal team.'

Twenty-four hours later, Mercedes and Channel Seven announced they had reached a confidential settlement in the case, saving any more costly court time. Some media speculated that the payout was as high as $1 million. It is believed Channel Seven spent more than $5 million on their defence.

Schapelle wept when told the news of her sister's victory, which was understandable as victories have been few and far between for Schapelle and her family since her 2004 arrest. Channel Seven settled with Rosleigh Rose over her defamation case on June 18, 2008. Lawyers for Channel Seven told Supreme Court Justice Lucy McCallum that they had offered Rosleigh a similar settlement to Mercedes for an undisclosed sum.

This ended a surprisingly happy period for the Corbys. However, like everything else that has been positive for them in recent years, it was short lived.

29.
Depression

WITH the Supreme Court victory still fresh, Rosleigh suddenly felt things were not right with Schapelle and her mother's instincts proved to be correct. She quizzed Michael Junior and Wayan, who had been looking after Schapelle's welfare while Mercedes had been living in Australia before and during the defamation case. 'They told me Schapelle was not eating or sleeping properly and had lost weight, but she had told them not to worry me or Merc,' Rosleigh told me in July 2008.

Rosleigh flew to Bali and found Schapelle had lost 12kg (26.5lb) and was down to 45kg (99lb). 'I made a fuss and I asked for a full range of medical tests to be carried out to find out if the problem was physical and they all came back fine,' she said. The doctors then discovered Schapelle was suffering from severe depression and she was taken to Sanglah Hospital.

'I think it was a combination of things, losing her dad, her step-dad, losing the last appeal and with Mercedes away from her for three months, it was all too much for her,' said Ros.

Mercedes also flew to Bali and slept in Schapelle's hospital room while Schapelle slowly recovered. At one stage after Schapelle had been in hospital for about a fortnight, she was photographed on July 2, 2008 going to a beauty salon under police guard for the first time in four years. It is believed she had a traditional Balinese body scrub, as well as hair treatment and a body massage. Some media tried to turn this into 'Schapelle goes on a shopping spree' story, but the salon and a mini mart she had also used were both within the hospital grounds and doctors thought the visit to the beauty salon would be good therapy for the depression.

Schapelle returned to Kerobokan after almost three weeks in hospital, after failing in an attempt to gain a transfer to a low security detention centre in another part of Bali which has a hospital attached to it. Prison authorities said only prisoners serving two years or less were eligible for the detention centre.

While she was in hospital, Australia's Channel 9 aired a two-part, four-hour special on Schapelle and the Corbys called 'Schapelle Corby—The Hidden Truth' that they billed as the definitive work on the 'long running Corby saga'.

It turned out to be the work of Sydney documentary film maker Janine Hosking that she had originally released in the US cinema market under the title of *Ganga Queen*. Ms Hosking told how she had spent three years of her life making this film and described it as an 'epic story'. Channel 9 boss David Gyngell said it was 'riveting, must-see television'.

Although she had won awards for her independent documentary making and appeared to have a good name in the business, I didn't think the documentary was fair. The Corby family was also disappointed that her documentary did not do justice to Schapelle's case.

This film had the potential to be a truly amazing documentary because of the access the Corbys had given Janine and her crew—instead it showed them at their worst.

Hosking spent three years gathering hundreds of hours of footage. There are so many important things that have happened to Schapelle that were not shown and I know a great deal of them were filmed. Instead we had a selection of clips.

Other scenes were shown, such as Michael junior and Schapelle joking about going to jail in Bangkok for a year then collecting $100,000. This would seem quite weird to most people, but it was just silly talk because both of them were so nervous at that time. Michael is fairly quiet and not a great conversationalist, but he has told me a few times how he misses joking around with his sister and this was just an attempt to try and lighten the mood and, even if wasn't very successful, that is the context in which it should be viewed. After numerous visits to Schapelle, I know how hard it can be to think of things to talk to her about and sometimes the conversations become quite trivial and irrelevant.

The documentary was particularly harsh on Mick Corby senior. What the program did not say at any point was that he was on heavy medication for his terminal cancer and had become extremely deaf and this combination contributed to scenes where he looked quite strange, especially when he was seen leaning forward right into the camera and yelling— that was Mick just simply trying to hear what was being said and yelling because of his acute deafness. The film crew spent so much time around the Corbys that they were well aware of his problems, but there was no allowance for that in the finished product.

'Hidden Truth' revisited the discredited Corby myth that Mercedes and Wayan owned a surf shop in Kuta or somewhere in Bali. This segment, however, did not dispute that nonsensical idea, rather it just left the myth hanging.

For the record again, Mercedes and Wayan do not and have never owned a surf shop in Bali. The closest connection to this idea is that Wayan was sponsored by a Kuta surf shop in the days when he was rated the No. 2 surfer in Indonesia some years ago. Otherwise, the program portrayed Mercedes and manipulative and even nasty, with Rasiah weighing in with his observations.

Mercedes has made no bones about the fact that her number one priority is Schapelle and she has never wavered from that path. Often, especially in the first 12 months, she found herself in an extremely alien environment, pressured by her legal team, then completely smothered by a voracious and often overly aggressive media on the other. It's no wonder that at times she lost control and came across as angry or confused. Yet the documentary chose to show her consistently out of control throughout its two-night screening.

My performance in the two-minute and four-second snippet interview, taken from several hours on camera in July 2005, was not terribly significant. I said many more interesting and important things during the full interview than was shown. In fact Hosking commented that I was the 'glue' at that stage because I was the only one who could put the whole thing together. Yet that did not come across in the largely pointless segment aired.

Then, on July 4, 2008, ABC TV's *Lateline* ran a story with a relative of Schapelle's claiming Mick Corby had been involved in the drug trade for 30 years and was a well known drug dealer in Mackay in the 1980s. The story had an on-camera interview with Mick's cousin Alan Trembath who said Mick Corby moved large amounts of marijuana throughout the Mackay area. He claimed on camera that Michael had offered him $80,000 to take a boat and bring 'a lot of marijuana' from Cedar Bay to Mackay. Cedar Bay near Cooktown made the news in 1976 when police raided hippie communes there and burnt homes.

For almost all the 1980s, the median house price in Brisbane was $50,000 so this supposed job as a drug courier, which didn't even entail crossing state borders let alone international ones, would have seen Trembath almost the owner of two houses. The going rate for a drug courier in the 1980s would not have even been $8000. The amount of marijuana being shipped would have needed to reach astronomical proportions to warrant paying the mule such a ridiculous sum.

But the ABC kept on and for the third time they filmed the woman whose evidence had been previously discredited in a Queensland court and was so garbled in the Supreme Court defamation case against Channel Seven that not one media outlet reported on it. The next morning ABC radio was running with the story.

The *Weekend Australian* on Saturday, July 5, 2008 had a balanced report which quoted a Queensland police spokesman as saying an investigation into statements made by an informant against Michael Corby had been investigated and were found to be unjustified. The spokesman said a full investigation had failed to link Michael Corby to any involvement in the drug trade.

That should have put the story to bed, but no, it was one of the headline items on National Nine *News* that night. No mention of the police statement surfaced in this report. Channel 9 interviewed Vasu Rasiah in Bali, calling him 'Schapelle's lawyer'. Yet Rasiah had been the case co-ordinator, was not a lawyer and had been removed from the case back in late-June 2005.

An AAP report took the Queensland police statement further with a spokesman saying: 'It's dead, over. It's an old story and I don't know why it's getting attention.' AAP also interviewed Alan Trembath's sister Lyn Lack, who discredited the statements made by her brother.

Rosleigh told me that Michael had never lived in Mackay and the sort of money being quoted was a joke. 'We were struggling in a Housing Commission home and Michael wasn't much better off,' she said. 'There is nothing we can do because only Schapelle and Michael's names were used in the reports and we can't take any legal action because Michael has passed away and Schapelle is locked up and they know they that full well.'

I've lost track of how many times this has happened, but at least the Queensland police were now on the record about Michael Corby.

They were called on again within days for another denial after a South Australian paper reported on July 12, 2008 that convicted drug trafficker Malcolm McCauley had claimed he supplied the marijuana Schapelle was caught with to her father Michael. McCauley had made headlines after police raided his Adelaide home and found pictures of him with Schapelle which were first claimed to have been taken before her arrest but were then found to be taken in Kerobokan.

Again, Rosleigh stated that she had met McCauley in the Secret Garden bar in Kuta where he told her that he was a supporter of her daughter and she invited him to come to the prison and meet Schapelle. He later spent 15 months in jail for his part in a drug syndicate which imported 100 kilograms of cannabis from South Australia to Queensland between 2004 and 2005. His claims about the late Michael Corby made headlines all over the country and had Rosleigh blaming herself all over again because she took him to meet Schapelle in the first place.

Fortunately a Queensland police spokesman weighed into the debate on July 13, 2008 and said police in that state had known about McCauley's claims for about 12 months. He said police had investigated those claims and found they were false.

'An investigation made by Queensland Police into statements made against Mick Corby found these statements to be unjustified,' the spokesman said.

'Queensland Police has no evidence to link Mick Corby with

involvement with the drug trade.'

It is a common phrase: 'Don't believe everything you read in the paper.' I hope readers of this book will remember not to automatically believe what they read or see about the Corbys in many sections of the Australia media in future, but rather look carefully and ask questions about what is really true.

30.
One day at a time, for twenty years

THIS is not the way I would have preferred to write this last chapter. I have been dreading doing it, because I just don't have a happy ending. I can't wave a magic wand and transport Schapelle back on to Tugun Beach at the southern end of the Gold Coast where she could walk with the sand between her toes and sit and watch a wonderful sunset, then go home, enjoy a refreshing shower and spend the night in a comfortable bed. Sadly none of that is going to happen in the near future.

For me, life has changed dramatically since I became involved in the Corby case. It has cost me a job that I loved at the *Gold Coast Bulletin* and who knows what the future holds. Sadly for Schapelle, her immediate future is Kerobokan prison.

When Schapelle's last appeal was turned down early in 2008, I was in dread for her future because I felt it had washed away any remaining shred of hope she was clinging to in that dark place. And without hope there is clearly nothing. But the words from outgoing Kerobokan Governor Ilham Djaya in April, 2008 about Schapelle gaining a higher 'rank', as explained in the previous chapter, were music to my ears.

Real hope was back firmly on the table and if Schapelle, who is a *Tamping* at present, can attain the higher rank of Pemuka (a person in charge of the *Tampings*) then she could be freed in five or six years without any loss of face by the Indonesians, which is a key factor in all of this, because it is their own system.

I don't think she should have served one day behind bars. The reality of Schapelle's present—four years on from her arrest—dictates that her family would accept anything less than the frightening alternative of 20 years in a Balinese prison.

I know Mercedes and her family do not want this to be Schapelle's only short to medium term option and they hope to free her sooner with her innocence acknowledged. The very sad reality is that I cannot see just how this is to be accomplished. Her mental health could be a major factor in her future and it's difficult to predict the role that might play.

Take away the possibility of becoming a *Pemuka* and Schapelle's future could only honestly be described as bleak. Looking for other answers, I feel that Prime Minister Kevin Rudd is a more compassionate man than his predecessor and if he could speak to the Indonesian leadership diplomatically, which is his forte, about Schapelle's case then maybe there would be some light at the end of the tunnel, but it is still a long tunnel.

In mid-August 2008, Schapelle was given three months off her sentence for Indonesian Independence Day. In 2007 she missed out on this reduction because she had been caught using a mobile phone in her cell. Having months cut from prisoners' sentences for good behaviour is the norm in the Indonesian penal system for Independence Day on August 17 and for Christians like Schapelle the same reductions are possible at Christmas.

Even so, it is a small reduction.

The Indonesian authorities are seemingly intransigent when it comes to clemency for people convicted of drug crimes, but given Australia's relationship with Indonesia, I have always felt that the right type of signal from an Australian leader should be able to open the right doors in this case. The oft-touted idea, in the media at least, of a prisoner exchange between Indonesia and Australia, is the bottom of the option pile in my opinion, because it could be at least nine years away for Schapelle and there would be no guarantees she would ever make such a list.

Re-opening the case in Indonesia, or in some international forum, has a snowflake's chance in hell of happening, let alone succeeding. The chances of ever finding out who put the drugs in Schapelle's bag fade further as each day passes, much as many of us beat ourselves up over that critical question.

I would favour a move to see professional negotiators employed to lobby Schapelle's case for clemency within the ranks of power in Indonesia. I envisage that this would be done in a respectful manner, in the Indonesian way and with no media attached to it at any stage. Such people exist and they are used in commercial scenarios to help various companies achieve a huge range of goals and outcomes in foreign countries and there is no reason why their method of operation could not be adapted to aid Schapelle's cause. Again I suspect this would be a lengthy process that would take some years to bear fruit.

It is where Schapelle is which part motivated me to write this book.

The other strong motivation came from a fierce and sustained anger at the manner in which Schapelle and the Corby family have been treated over the past four years. No other Australian family I can think of has ever endured such a painful and public flogging.

I am so tired of people telling me they (the Corby family) are all grubs, that 'the brother did it', that the whole family is 'into drugs' or 'deals drugs' or, in extreme cases, to be told 'you are part of their drug dealing operation and have been involved for years'. Ninety-nine times out of one hundred, these people know nothing about the Corbys, this case or anything remotely connected to it.

And so it was time to tell the truth behind the headlines and so-called documentaries.

Schapelle sits in her Balinese cage, totally unable to defend herself from anyone who wants to take advantage of her situation. The road ahead remains rocky for Schapelle, but it is not impassable. I believe this book has shed light on the real Corbys and the wrongs they have all endured since the fateful day in October, 2004.

I hope that those who have read this book will at least look more favourably on Schapelle and her family in the future. I have no doubt of her innocence and I implore you to now consider it.

More than that, become angry that an innocent is detained for false reasons in Bali. And never, ever forget Schapelle Leigh Corby, an Aussie woman bravely surviving a 'Groundhog Day' of absolute horror and pain in a foreign land, incarcerated for a crime she did not commit. Free Schapelle Corby.

THE FACTS
and the MYTHS

Why did Schapelle go to Bali?

Did Schapelle travel regularly to Bali?
No. Her last visit before her arrest was four years earlier.

Why was Schapelle going to Bali in 2004?
For a holiday break from caring for her terminally ill father Mick and to celebrate her sister Mercedes 30th birthday.

Why was Mercedes already in Bali?
Mercedes and her Indonesian husband Wayan had taken their two children to Bali so the children could have a taste of Balinese culture before Wayan junior started school in Australia on the Gold Coast at the beginning of 2005.

Why did Schapelle take her own boogie-board to Bali?
She liked to use her own board, and didn't want to hire or buy one.

Does Mercedes husband Wayan own a surf shop?
No, he never has. The closest connection is that he was sponsored by a surf shop in Kuta several years ago when he was ranked the number-two surfer in Indonesia.

The airports

Do bags get checked or photographed when they are transferred between domestic and international flights in Australia?
Yes, they are scanned but not checked for vegetable matter.

Was Schapelle's Corby's bags checked or photographed between the domestic flight from Brisbane and the international flight to Bali?
No.

Why weren't they?

There isn't any proof that they were. The surveillance records from Brisbane were erased within 72 hours of the flight. The security cameras were out of order in Sydney when her bags went through.

What about weight? Weren't the bags weighed before they left Sydney for Bali and then when they arrived there?

The bags were weighed collectively in Brisbane, and not individually. There is no individual bag weight for the boogie-board bag. They were not weighed in Sydney. They were not weighed in Bali. There was no individual bag weight for Schapelle's luggage.

The drugs

What was found in Schapelle's boogie-board bag?

A 4.1kg (9lb) bag of marijuana wrapped in two bags—an inner bag and an outer bag.

Would Schapelle and her travelling companions, Alyth, Katrine and her brother James, have known about the severe penalties for drug offences in Indonesia?

Nobody who has been through Denpasar Airport would be under any confusion about the penalties for drug carries. It is written in bold red writing that the death penalty will be applied to drug carriers. The family had travelled to Bali for Mercedes wedding and would have seen clearly the signs in the airport.

Whose fingerprints were found on the two bags of marijuana?

No-one's because they were never tested for fingerprints.

Where did the marijuana come from in the first place?
The drugs Schapelle was found with were never tested for place of origin. They were burnt in March 2006 and nobody will ever know the answer to that question.

Did Schapelle refuse to agree to a DNA test on the marijuana?
This is false. In the presence of the Australian Consul-General she agreed to the AFP testing back in December 2004. But the Indonesian authorities never asked the AFP to carry out any tests.

Was it hydroponic marijuana?
TV images and photos suggest it may have been but it has never been proven.

Do Australians buy hydroponic drugs in Bali in preference to the local ones?
There is no evidence to support this claim.

What was the value of the drugs in the bag to a drug buyer in Bali?
The drugs would have cost someone approximately $32,000 to buy in Australia. The same quantity of drugs by weight was worth around $4,500 in Bali at that time.

The Corby family

Does Michael Corby have a drug conviction?

No, he received a small fine after police raided a party in the 1970s and found a small quantity of marijuana at the party in the days before his children were born. There is no conviction recorded against his name.

Are the Corby family drug dealers?

Despite police investigations, there is no evidence that any of the family have been involved in any drug dealing, trafficking or smuggling. There is a Queensland police statement to that effect.

What about Schapelle's half brother James? Would he have smuggled the drugs into Bali?

James was 17 at the time. It is hard to imagine where a 17-year old would have got hold of $32,000 worth of marijuana, or that anyone would entrust that amount of marijuana to a person of his age.

Is Schapelle covering up and doing time in jail for another person's drug crime?

She has repeatedly stated that she would not do jail time for anyone else, not even a family member.

The Australian government

Did the Australian government help the family?
Yes, they paid the legal bill of Vasu Rasiah, the Bali Law Chambers, of around $100,000.

Could they have done more?
They could have sent a government official to give evidence at Schapelle's trial about the extent of drug-related problems in Australian airports.

The case against Schapelle

What was the main evidence in her case from the prosecution?
The prosecution case rested entirely on the Custom's officer's statement that Schapelle admitted that the drugs were hers when she came through Customs. Schapelle never admitted the drugs were hers—only that the bag was hers.

Would Schapelle have been convicted in Australia?
In Australia her case would have caused serious doubt because of the lack of evidence as to the ownership of the drugs. There were no fingerprint tests, no testing of the drugs, no camera evidence, no baggage handling evidence. The likely outcome is that the lack of evidence would have found her not guilty.

What was her sentence?
Twenty years—one of the largest sentences in Indonesian legal history for a marijuana offence at that time.

The lawyers

Who were Schapelle's lawyers?

Lily Sri Rahaya Lubis, Erwin Siregar and Hotman Paris Hutapea.

Who is Vasu Rasiah?

Vasu Rasiah is the owner of the Bali Law Chambers, who employed Lily and Erwin. He is Sri Lankan born with an Australian passport.

Is he a lawyer?

No. He claims to have Engineering and English degrees from Australia and described himself as 'case coordinator'. He was dismissed from the case.

Who is Ron Bakir?

Ron Bakir is a businessman and entrepreneur, from the Gold Coast.

What did he do?

He was involved with the case from late February 2005 to July 2005, a total of five months. He claimed to have funded Schapelle's legal case and fought for her release but he was not invited by Schapelle or her family to do that. No proof has been found to support the degree of his financial involvement.

Who is Robin Tampoe?

A Gold Coast lawyer.

What did he do?

He worked on the case with Bali Law Chambers, although he was not invited by Schapelle or her family to take that role.

Who was Hotman Paris Hutapea?

Leading Indonesian lawyer who was brought in to run the appeals.

What did he do?

He got the case reopened and five years taken off her original sentence. This was overturned in the final appeal in Jakarta.

Money

Does it cost money for Schapelle to be in Kerobokan?

Yes. She has to rent her cell, buy edible food, water, pay for her mail to be delivered and sent, pay for doctor and dentist treatments, pay for guards to take her to and from visits. If you don't pay, inevitably you die in Kerobokan.

What does Schapelle's family do for her now?

They supply all her food, water, clothing, toiletries, medicines, bedding, books, and moral and psychological support. This is at least bi-weekly and requires a member of the family to be in Bali permanently.

Has the Corby family made any money out of her case?

Through legal victories in the defamation case against Channel Seven, Mercedes and Rosleigh settled their cases for an undisclosed amount. It is unclear what if anything was made from the sales of *My Story*.

The future

Does Schapelle have any more legal options?

There are no more legal options. The best chance for Schapelle is through the Indonesian penal system by promotion for good behaviour.

The media

How has the media coverage affected this case?

The exposure by the media of Schapelle and her family in this case has been detrimental to her and may have contributed to her inflated sentence. The media focus on digging up alleged 'Corby dirt' impacts on her chances for good behaviour promotion and continues to do so.

Visit the New Holland website

www.newholland.com.au

To sign up and receive the monthly
New Holland newsletter

www.newholland.com.au/newsletter

To view the Schapelle video and online discussion:

www.youtube.com/newhollandpublishers

Also available from New Holland

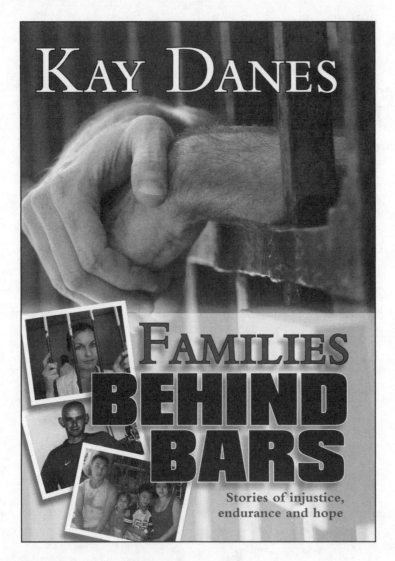

Families Behind Bars
Kay Danes

ISBN: 9781741106763

Coming in 2009

Standing Ground

An Australian couple's struggle against a Communist Regime

Kay Danes

ISBN: 9781741107579

On December 23, 2000, when her husband was abducted from his office in Laos by secret police, Kay Danes gathered their two youngest children and on advice from the Australian Embassy, headed to the border, only to be intercepted by the same ruthless police.

Forced into a nightmare of epic proportions, Kay was wrenched from her children and sent to an undisclosed location. It was then that her real nightmare began.

Held hostage and at the mercy of a paranoid Communist regime, Kay and her husband endured torture and ill-treatment and witnessed unspeakable human rights violations.

Standing Ground is the story of her courage and struggle to survive, while the Australian government tried desperately to have her and Kerry freed.